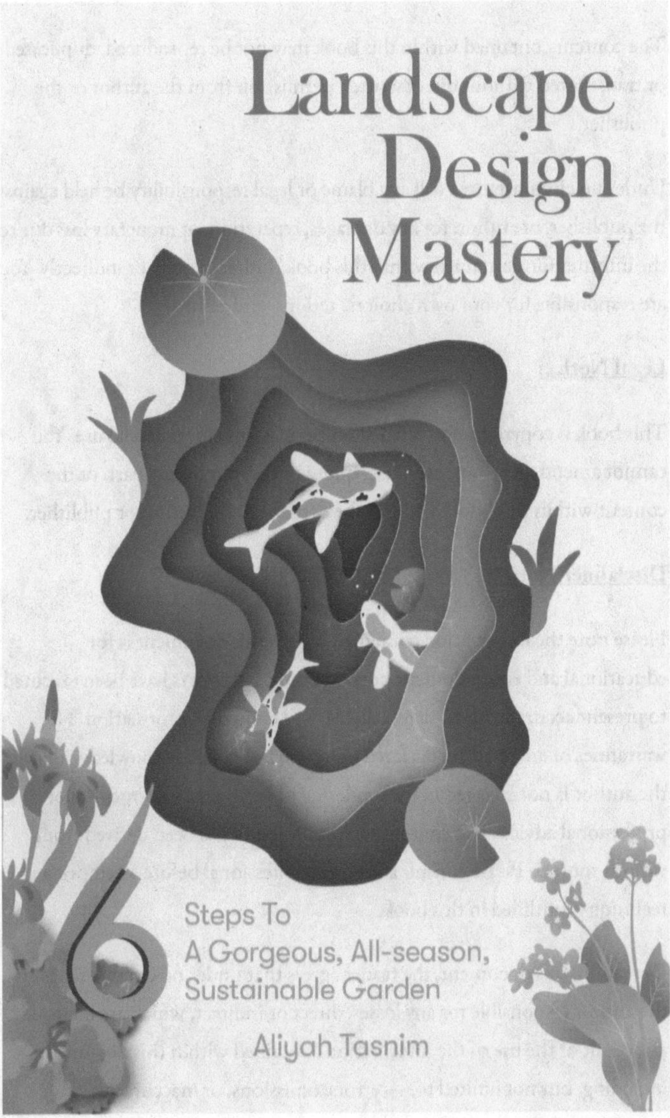
Landscape Design Mastery
6 Steps To A Gorgeous, All-season, Sustainable Garden
Aliyah Tasnim

Copyright © 2023 by Aliyah Tasnim

All rights reserved.

The content contained within this book may not be reproduced, duplicated or transmitted without direct written permission from the author or the publisher.

Under no circumstances will any blame or legal responsibility be held against the publisher, or author, for any damages, reparation, or monetary loss due to the information contained within this book. Either directly or indirectly. You are responsible for your own choices, actions, and results.

Legal Notice:

This book is copyright protected. This book is only for personal use. You cannot amend, distribute, sell, use, quote or paraphrase any part, or the content within this book, without the consent of the author or publisher.

Disclaimer Notice:

Please note the information contained within this document is for educational and entertainment purposes only. All efforts have been executed to present accurate, up-to-date, reliable, and complete information. No warranties of any kind are declared or implied. Readers acknowledge that the author is not engaged in the rendering of legal, financial, medical or professional advice. The content within this book has been derived from various sources. Please consult a licensed professional before attempting any techniques outlined in this book.

By reading this document, the reader agrees that under no circumstances is the author responsible for any losses, direct or indirect, which are incurred as a result of the use of the information contained within this document, including, but not limited to, — errors, omissions, or inaccuracies.

First edition 2023. Book cover by Aliyah Tasnim.

LANDSCAPE DESIGN MASTERY

Contents

Introduction	1
About the Author	8
1. The Nine Principles Of Landscape Design	11
2. How To Avoid Disastrous Design	32
3. Brilliant Beginnings: Getting Going	50
4. A Climate-Conscious Garden	73
5. Sustainable Solutions in Garden Design	113
6. Delightful Design Ideas For All Budgets	140
7. Conclusion	168
Bibliography	174

Introduction

Have you ever considered your ideal garden an unattainable, unrealistic, dream-world fantasy? What if I told you that your ultimate dream garden already exists? You would probably think I was crazy. Or delusional. Or both. But the fact is, it does exist. Inside your head, as a fantasy. Disappointed? Don't be, because I'm here to make that fantasy a reality. By the end of this book, you will see your dream garden translated into a landscape plan and, eventually, in real life, where your old, mundane garden used to be. If only you knew that everything you have ever wanted is on its way to you. All you have to do is read this book and discover how to create your dream garden using the steps I will provide you with.

Designing a garden can seem like endless hard work, painstaking hours of planning and fretting about what goes where. Unfortunately, you're no stranger to these soul-destroying, limiting thoughts:

"My garden is an eyesore, and I'm not skilled enough to do anything about it."

"Fixing my garden into something I am proud of is completely out of my budget, and I can't afford to have anything nice".

"My garden is too small/too big to design, and I don't know where/how to begin."

"My garden is doomed to be a mulchy mess because I will never have proper drainage."

"Having a nice garden requires high maintenance, and I'm just not up for that commitment."

"I will never be able to host gatherings, events, or parties in my backyard because it's too ugly, unfit for purpose, and always will be."

"Nothing will ever grow in that shady patch by the fence."

"No plants will ever survive in the full-sun conditions in my backyard."

"I live in a desert climate, so I can't have a nice garden with plants that grow. I'm doomed to cacti and arid-looking grass that even cows wouldn't graze".

"The climate I live in won't allow me to have plants that last all year round."

"I'll never have privacy in my backyard because the neighbours can see in from all angles no matter what I try to do."

Sound familiar? Well, I've got news for you: how you view anything depends on your perception. So, follow the six simple steps in this book. Then, your dream garden will come quickly to you and be part of your new awesome reality, and these thoughts will never enter your mind again.

I understand how daunting this task feels. You go to the kitchen every morning to make tea or coffee and glance out the window. There's nothing. No blooming flowers to greet you, no water feature to make the neighbours stare (or want to stare), and not even a tiny tree to give your garden some character. There are even "unusable" areas that have been drenched from excessive rainfall, creating a squelchy mess every time someone walks there. You certainly can't host parties or gatherings here in this abomination of a backyard.

It lacks any sense of design whatsoever. Nothing looks back at you except a vast expanse of boring, discoloured lawn. There are brown and yellow patches where the sun has scorched it. So how do you break up that massive central area and make it enjoyable to look at? Why can you see the whole ugly yard at once, and how on earth can you get some privacy just the way it is? And what about summer nights, when you fantasise about relaxing outdoors with some excellent garden illumination but realise you can't because the outside looks like a black hole? It seems like a chasm, a neverending expanse of nothingness...

"WHERE DO I BEGIN?!" I hear you, don't worry. We will explore how to turn your garden from "meh" to "YEAH!" Your neighbours are looking at your garden with disgust and even pity. You don't blame them; your yard's current state makes you feel ashamed of yourself and your property.

Well, no more! With this book as your guide, you will learn how to utilise the space in your garden to create garden ENVY. Your garden will be the new talk of the block. It will turn heads. People will DOUBLE-TAKE to get a good look at it.

You will have the most gorgeous garden you can think of. It will be beautiful and inviting, perfect for hosting guests and relaxing. There will be areas of seclusion and privacy where no one else can see you. You will have utilised every last inch of your garden so that everything works in harmony from a design and functional point of view. You will have a colourful garden that works with the seasons and your climate, giving back to nature instead of taking away from it. And this will all be within your budget.

By the end of this book, you will be a garden wizard, knowing what to plant and where. Annuals, perennials, grasses, succulents - you name it, you'll know exactly where to put it. And they will flourish. You'll learn exactly what your garden needs to make this happen, so you will never have to worry about seeing a bunch of dead, failing plants in your backyard ever again.

You will walk down the new, stylish walkway that YOU PLANNED to a secluded spot in your garden and chill in the warm breeze. You will have a focal point and that water feature you always wanted. And yes, YOU WILL HAVE THE DRAINAGE YOU'VE ALWAYS NEEDED.

Your landscape will be luscious and brimming with life. Even the local wildlife will spread good gossip about your little oasis.

You will have the garden you have always dreamed of. Every morning you will look outside your window and squeal with delight. Your eyes will water with the marvel of your creation. You will be so proud of your garden that you want to go out into the street and yell "PARTY AT MINE AFTER WORK!" every week to show it off (unless that sounds like a complete nightmare to you, and you would instead enjoy your garden yourself). And I will be the one to get you there, all done sustainably.

I will walk you through the entire process, step by step, until you have become the master of your garden. You will make your garden work for you, not the other way around.

You will learn precisely the nine principles that make up excellent landscape design, how to apply them to your garden, and how to avoid the opposite. Second, you will finally understand what it takes to get started on your current blank garden canvas and all the considerations to make before you start designing. Thirdly, you'll never have to worry about placing vegetation in the wrong place again because I've got you covered with suggestions and what to look out for. I even give you landscape design ideas for your garden if you live in a desert climate and ideas for when the weather becomes wet and windy. Finally, if that's not enough, I will also reveal how to weatherproof your garden.

Of course, part of the package is a sustainable garden; you'll learn how to work with nature so your garden's mini-ecosystems can thrive. You'll also be able to attract pollinators easily, should you wish to. And don't worry about money because I cover that too - whether you have a high or low budget, you can trust that I have ideas for your new garden.

About the Author

I have had an interest in the natural world since childhood. I loved spending time outdoors in nature (and still do), never fully knowing all the benefits this had on my mental, physical, and spiritual well-being. I was taught to respect the planet and its natural resources, giving back to the environment whenever possible. My interest in sustainability began after studying Geography at GCSE and A-level, where I was exposed to how natural systems worked. As a child, I always loved art and creativity. So I pursued this passion by studying design at GCSE and University. I completed a three-year degree in Urban Landscape Architecture at Ravensbourne University London to further my understanding of eco-friendly and sustainable design, gaining First Class Honours. During the period of my writing this book, I was working in sustainability at BAFTA albert.

My high achievements in education and career are due to my passion for creating beautiful, functional landscapes considering current climate conditions. I have been studying both design and sustainability for eight years.

I am writing this book because I have first-hand experience designing landscapes on live briefs for real-life clients. In addition, I have a fantastic knowledge of sustainable landscape design that I cannot wait to share with you because I know it can help you solve your garden frustrations (while contributing to a better planet overall).

Helping you achieve your perfect garden matters deeply to me because what you are about to learn extensively impacts climate change, an issue I care most deeply about. Designing sustainable gardens that work with your climate benefits you and the rest of the planet. I grew up in London, where green space is poorly and frustratingly used (most of the time). As a former landscape design student, it bothers me to see space not utilized efficiently, effectively, or sustainably.

I have a passion for beautiful, sustainable landscape design and an understanding of design principles to make your garden work for you. I also live on a budget, so I understand the pain of being financially constricted. However, you can still have the garden of your dreams on a tight budget. Read on to find out exactly how to design a gorgeous garden that works for you, starting with the nine core principles of landscape design.

1
The Nine Principles Of Landscape Design

To create a garden you love, you must first understand landscape design basics. Understanding this will ensure that everything goes in the right place and has a purpose for being there.

Landscaping is a process that can transform your property from boring to extraordinary. You may define it as adding interest to an area by using plants and structures and manipulating terrain. By this, I mean changing the shape of your land through various means, including terracing, grading, backfilling, and mounding. By structures, I am referring to hardscape elements (which will be covered in depth later on in this book) such as walls, fences, a patio, and other built features.

Design principles help designers organise their landscape elements for an aesthetically pleasing result. In addition to making a nice-looking garden, following these principles also aid in achieving mental and physical comfort. People naturally feel more at ease in a landscape with order and repetition. Proportion, unity, repetition, and order principles can achieve a harmonious landscape composition. Using one helps to apply the others, as all are linked. Mental comfort also comes from seeing a unified landscape with the correct use of proportion.

***

Proportion

There are two types: relative and absolute. Relative refers to the size of an object in relation to others, whereas absolute proportion means an object's size. You must always consider the human scale when designing landscapes, as we are the primary users of it. People feel safer in tinier open areas like terraces and patios and feel at ease within structures that have elements reminiscent of a ceiling, such as an arbour. Garden elements that are a happy medium between indoors and outdoors are an excellent choice for comfort; anything that implies enclosure while letting in light and sky views makes people feel at ease. Keep this in mind when deciding on structures, plants, and ornaments.

You have a balanced composition when the house, plants, and people are proportionate. However, ensuring the same amount of open and planted space can also achieve balance. You can emphasise certain plants by choosing a mix of larger and smaller species. Using similar-sized plants creates a rhythm as size is seemingly repeated and constant. Hardscape should be proportional to your home; for example, a perfect patio is big enough to entertain guests but small enough to fit the house's scale.

Unity

Unity is when garden elements are linked together, creating consistency in composition. The opposite of unity is having scattered plants and unrelated ornaments in your garden. Emphasising elements in the garden automatically makes them an important feature and captures the eye, making them a focal point. Having these focal points helps to guide the eye and influence circulation. They can also act as a distraction to create more privacy in another area of your garden.

Interconnection is when various features touch - the key is a seamless linkage between elements. An example of this in a landscape is the continuation of a pathway.

Features grouped in odd numbers, such as threes, fives, or sevens, are more visually balanced and seem more strongly unified. In addition, odd numbers enable height variations in the groups, making them look more attractive. In contrast, even numbers are visually divided more easily by the eye.

To bring purpose to your garden design, keep it simple and non-chaotic. You can achieve this by thoughtfully eliminating unnecessary features while preserving the garden's character.

Repetition

Repetition is when you use elements repeatedly to make a sequence or patterns in the landscape. Simple repetition uses the same plant across the garden, for example. Although, repetition can sometimes use the same colour, form, or texture throughout the landscape. This creates rhythm. However, too much repetition will make a landscape look boring, while too little can confuse the viewer. Alternation can add interest to repetition. Alternation means adding a tiny change in the sequence at regular intervals. An example is using a circular form after every four square forms along your garden. You may use inversion (a different type of alternation) in repetition and works by being the direct opposite of the sequence of elements; for example, every fifth plant in a series of pyramidal plants is one vase-shaped plant.

Gradually changing a feature's characteristics along a sequence is another way to add interest to repetition. For example, a square form could become progressively bigger or smaller along the length of the garden or use different sizes of grasses. You can also use gradation in texture and colour, such as a coarse texture transitioning into a finer texture or flowers transitioning from light to dark shades of purple.

Material can also be used consistently throughout the garden to create unity, but changing the colour, size, or texture adds variety. Repetition can appear more evident in hardscapes because manufactured materials are made with specific dimensions.

Order

One can achieve order through balance, which refers to the spatial layout in design. Balance is the idea of equal visual weight and attraction and is affected by colour, texture, form, and size. Both asymmetrical and symmetrical designs can achieve balance. For example, you can achieve order in your garden by grouping elements or arranging them around a central spot.

Symmetrical balance is when objects mirror each other's position, i.e. the same trees, plants, and ornaments are used on both sides of the garden. This spatial concept has been used in many gardens throughout history to create formal gardens.

Asymmetrical balance is when both sides of the garden carry the equal visual weight of different forms, textures, or colours. Using asymmetrical balance is usually part of an informal garden style. It is achieved by using plant masses with similar visual weight. You can also include structures and garden ornaments in your mass. Use large features, bright colours, and coarse textures sparingly for balance as they have higher visual weight. Simultaneously, use a higher amount of smaller elements, muted colours, and fine textures.

When viewing a landscape, the objects closest to the viewer appear to have a higher visual weight. So to achieve perspective balance, use larger objects, coarser textures, and brighter colours in the background. However, you can choose to make the foreground or background the dominant.

Design elements are visual qualities that people see when looking at an area. Visual qualities have power over how people react to a place, so you want to evoke positive emotions to allow people to enjoy the space naturally. The first element we will explore together is line.

Line

One can use line in a multitude of ways to create an infinite number of patterns, forms, and shapes. Line is, therefore, a potent design tool. A form's outline (such as a tree against the sky), where two materials' edges meet (such as grass meeting a patio), and a lengthy linear feature is what form lines in a landscape. Line also influences the eye and body movement of a person. Therefore, landscape designers use lines to control movement, establish dominance, and create spaces and a cohesive theme within the landscape. Common lines include hardscape, path lines, fence, sod lines, and bedlines. The purposes of these lines vary, and they can have different characteristics.

For example, bedlines are when plant bed edges meet another surface material, such as groundcover, turf, gravel, and pavers. They visually connect plant material to the hardscape and the house. Hardscape lines are made by the edges of the hardscape and can make built structures stand out. In general, lines define softscape and hardscape areas on a plan and help to draw out forms.

Line properties affect people's emotional and physical responses to the landscape. There are four main types of lines, the first being straight lines; these can be structural, often creating symmetry in the garden and can lead the eye to a focal point. They often create a sense of formality and are typically found in hardscape edges. Curved lines, on the other hand, create an informal, natural design that often results in asymmetry and a relaxed ambience. In addition, curved lines can create hidden views, adding a sense of mystery to the space.

Vertical lines move the viewer's eye upwards, creating the illusion of a larger space. One can use vertical lines to emphasise a garden element. Examples of these in a landscape include tall structures (natural or artificial) such as trees or an arbour. Horizontal lines can also trick the eye into believing in a bigger space. Spatially, they can divide or unite a space. Low lines are found in small hedges, walkways, and low garden walls.

Form

The following landscape design principle is form which you can find in plants and hardscapes. It is often the factor that determines the garden style and organises the landscape. Typically, it dominates the visual elements of the garden. Form can be split into two main categories: formal and informal. Geometric forms are known to be formal, with shapes such as circles, polygons, and squares. In contrast, informal forms are natural, fragmented, and organic edges. Examples of the latter include plant silhouettes and negative space between plants.

Circular forms can either be whole circles, semi-circles, or circle segments. These forms can also be manipulated into elliptical shapes, creating variety and interest. Circular forms are a strong design choice because they can highlight a focal point and connect forms.

Square forms are easy to construct in many built features, such as stepping stones, bricks, and tiles. The square form can also be used for repetition (another principle we will come to later) to create unique patterns, like a grid or overlapping and new complex forms. They have solid and definitive edges, unlike circles.

Polygons also have straight edges but can have irregular angles, enabling them to form interesting shapes. A triangle is an example of a polygon. However, use polygonal forms with caution! Simplicity is often best here because the forms can become complex.

Naturalistic forms are usually in mimicry of nature. You can find them in meandering lines like rivers and streams in natural formations. These form types are great for pathways and plant beds. The curved nature of the line makes it a wonderful way to add mystery to a garden by hiding viewpoints and creating curiosity. They seamlessly guide people around corners to discover new spaces.

Organic edges are irregular and often rough because they mimic natural material. Organic lines are usually found in rock gardens and can be created purposely on hardscape edges.

Fragmented edges usually create gradually disappearing borders on patios and walkways. These edges can appear scattered; examples of these edges include pavers and stones.

Plant forms are created when individual plants are well established, but you may also find them in plant masses. For example, many plants grouped will create a new form different to an individual plant's form. Of course, having a contrasting form within a plant mass will allow for a focal point, so you should use high contrasts with care; too many will look messy and chaotic. Natural forms should dominate most of the composition in a successful plant mass. It would be best to limit the number of well-trimmed forms. An easy fact to remember is that vertical forms add height while horizontal forms add width.

Tree forms have different shapes, from round, oval, columnar, vase-shaped, pyramidal, and weeping. The differing forms are essential for their unique visual appeal and function. For instance, a round or oval tree is the right choice if you want to create shade. In contrast, a good privacy tree usually has a columnar or pyramidal form. A weeping tree makes an excellent focal point.

Shrub forms are irregular, spiky, vase-shaped, arching, mounding, rounded, cascading, and upright. When choosing shrub forms, consider whether it will be used as a mass or as an individual; spreading and mounding shrubs are better in a mass, while cascading and vase-shaped shrubs can be appreciated as standalone specimens.

Different groundcover forms include matting, clumping, sprawling, spreading, and short spikes. Most groundcovers look better in masses as they are typically tiny, giving them a small individual impact.

To recap, people tend to recognise the outlines and silhouettes of features, making form a powerful design tool. Pattern is the most basic way to organise a landscape and can be created using the repetition of a form. Also, forms can determine whether a garden is formal or informal; typical formal gardens use straight edges from geometric shapes, while informal gardens use natural and organic forms. Using one or two contrasting forms is excellent for emphasis. Still, all other forms should be similar for a sense of unity.

Texture

Texture refers to the coarseness or fineness of a plant or hardscape surface, such as buildings, walkways, walls, and patios. It provides variety and contrast and adds interest to a landscape. You may use the shape and size of a plant's leaves to determine its texture. Typical plant textures are coarse, medium, and fine. Coarse textures capture attention, while fine textures give the illusion of a larger space. Rough textures do the opposite, making spaces feel smaller.

Large, irregular-edged leaves; variegated colours; thick twigs and branches; and bold forms all create coarse texture. Agaves, hollies, palms, and hydrangeas are all examples of course-textured plants. Coarse hardscape textures include stone and brick that have been rough-cut or rough-finished.

Small foliage, thin stems, leaves, branches; vines; and delicate flowers are all fine-textured. Plants with this texture include ferns, grasses, and Japanese maples. Fine-textured hardscapes include stone, ceramic, or wood with smooth surfaces; glass ornaments. Water with a fine spray and smooth water is considered to have fine textures.

Most plants have medium texture, characterised by leaves of medium size and smooth edges, with typically mounding or rounded forms. Medium textures are great at linking and unifying coarse and fine-textured plants. Examples of medium-textured plants include agapanthus, viburnum, and camellia. Hardscape elements with this texture include finished woods and flagstone pavers.

Texture is a vital landscape design principle as it influences the perception of scale and distance. Use fine textures to outline the perimeter of your garden, medium textures in the middle, and coarse textures closest to the viewer to create the illusion of a larger space. Use coarse textures on the perimeter and fine textures closest to the viewer to make a space feel smaller. Fine textures are small and tend to fade into the landscape, whereas the detail of coarse textures makes plants appear closer.

Colours can affect how textures are perceived; bolder choices look coarser, while subtle, muted colours flatten textures. Designers often draw a texture study on paper, helping to decide on plant arrangement. You can depict textures using different line weights and shading techniques.

Colour

Colour is another element that adds interest to a landscape; it is usually the main focus in a garden, being the most noticeable element of landscape design. Using a colour wheel to create colour schemes is the best way to start planning colour in your garden. The colour wheel consists of three primary colours (red, blue, and yellow); three secondary colours created after mixing two primary colours (purple, orange, and green); and six tertiary colours made after mixing adjacent primary and secondary colours (red-orange, yellow-orange, red-violet, blue-violet, yellow-green, and blue-green). The wheel helps explain the relationship between colours and how they should be used. There are three basic colour schemes.

1. **Monochromatic:** A colour scheme comprising of one colour only. Regarding landscaping, this refers to one colour other than the existing green foliage. An all-green garden uses texture and form to create interest. However, one colour can have many hues and shades, adding interest. An example of a garden using monochromatic colour is white flowers, white foliage, white ornaments, and a white hardscape.

2. **Analogous** schemes use three adjacent colours on the colour wheel: blue, blue-violet, and violet. This colour scheme is also known as harmonious because the colours are related; they are usually comprised of secondary and two tertiary colours, meaning their properties are similar.

3. **Complementary**: Two opposing colours on the colour wheel make a complementary scheme. Common choices are red and green, blue and orange, and yellow and purple. These schemes all have high contrasts and are often found in nature (i.e. flowers).

Colour in the garden comes mainly from plants and hardscapes. In plants, many components add colour, including petals, foliage, fruit, and bark. Green foliage dominates due to its volume compared to flowers, but other colours contrast vividly with the green, grabbing attention. Garden colour changes as the seasons change; summer colours are usually brighter, while winter colours are darker, involving more foliage. The intensity of the summer sun can also make colours appear more saturated compared to winter's feeble light when colours appear dimmer.

Colours in hardscapes (rocks, paving, wood, garden furniture, built elements) are often naturally muted, including shades of brown, grey, and pale yellow. However, you may find brighter colours in artificial elements that have been painted, such as furniture, ceramic containers, sculptures, and ornaments.

Colour is also known for influencing emotions, scale, light quality, balance, and creating emphasis. Colours also have a temperature; warm colours evoke excitement, energy, and happiness and are successful in party areas. They are usually found in reds and can make a space feel smaller. Cool colours are found in blues and evoke calmness, serenity, and relaxation, with the power to make spaces feel larger. Thus, consider what time of day you will utilise your yard when choosing a colour scheme.

Bright colours are great for focal points; for example, a 'pop' of colour such as a vivid yellow contrasts highly with other colours and should therefore be used carefully. Remember this tip: a small amount of intense colour is as visually compelling as a large amount of a muted colour. As colour is a temporary and ever-changing element, you should use it to accentuate texture and form in the garden. A colour study in plan view is also helpful before design begins to help use colour effectively in your garden.

Visual Weight

Visual weight is the idea that some compositional garden elements are more important than others; some elements are more noticeable, while others blend into the background. Background features increase the overall cohesiveness of the design by linking (high visual weight) features together and providing the eye with a resting place. Without background features, the garden would look chaotic as the eye would simultaneously be drawn to too many features. You can create high visual weight with a group of plants that have one or some of these characteristics: diagonal lines; unusual or upright forms; bright colour; bold texture; and grand in size. Conversely, you may find low visual weight in opposing features such as low forms, fine textures, dull colours, and horizontal lines.

***

How to apply them

Now you know the basic principles and elements, you can begin to apply them to your garden. A good starting point is finding an existing garden design you like and examining how the principles have been used in that design. The best way to make your own fabulous design is by using other successful garden designs as inspiration and then adapting the ideas to suit your garden and site conditions.

You must find your sense of style to make your garden your own. To do this, think about other landscapes that bring you joy. Study the ones you love and note down the features and plants they use. Try also to identify which design elements and principles they use (colour, form, texture) and how they use balance, rhythm, and line. You don't have to go far to find landscape inspiration - the ones in your local area will do. In fact, it is often more helpful to stay within the neighbourhood to gather ideas. We subconsciously want to fit in with our neighbours since it comforts us.

However, suppose you did want to explore outside your neighbourhood. In that case, good sources of inspiration include local botanical gardens, displays at local nurseries, and demonstration gardens (which have pleasantly grouped plant arrangements). As these are all local to you, the growing conditions of these plants will be similar to that of your garden. Therefore, you can use the same combinations of plants (providing your garden has the right amount of sun and shade).

Another way to find your style is through magazines and books with garden or landscape images. Notice what you like and don't like about the designs. You can often substitute hardscape and plant materials to suit your region with those that contain similar characteristics to achieve the desired effect. It helps to visualise where your selected features will go in your garden. It is ok to choose ideas from several gardens to create your unique design. Remember that gardens in magazines are there because they have outstanding designs, so consider your (and your contractor's) abilities, adjusting the plan where appropriate.

Hardscape Vs Softscape

What is hardscape? It is anything in the landscape that is not alive, such as stone, metal, concrete, and bricks. You can also think of hardscape as anything artificial, which is often the most expensive part of your garden. Softscape is, therefore, all the living elements of your garden, including grass, trees, plants, shrubs, flowers, and soil. These are natural. A good garden design combines a balance of hardscape and softscape.

In gardens, hardscape is patios, walkways, arbours, furniture, fire pits, and retaining walls. Although in rock gardens, the rocks look natural but are a part of the hardscape. Other hardscaping materials not mentioned include wood, tile, and pavers. Hardscape is often seen as the garden's practical elements as they prioritise the human user. Fences for privacy, retaining walls to prevent soil erosion, creating a planting area or transforming slopes into flat areas, and walkways for safe passage and direction are all examples of practical hardscape elements. However, hardscapes can be used as focal points too. Wooden arbours, fire pits, fountains, and stone columns are all examples. Hardscape elements also have the power to immerse people into the landscape using designated areas. For example, patios and gazebos are great for relaxation and observance; pergolas are great for shelter; walkways are essential for directing the circulation of visitors.

As softscape is all-natural, you should consider seasonal changes, such as heat and frost, when planning your design. Many landscapes use seasonal change to their advantage, capturing each season's unique colour and character and using some plants that last throughout the year. Unlike hardscaping, softscaping requires regular maintenance to keep its beauty constant. Maintenance could include weeding, mowing, drainage, grading, planting, watering, pruning, and fertilising. If this sounds like more work than it's worth, think again. Many softscaping elements are low-maintenance and will add natural beauty to your yard.

Now we know what they are, let's learn about the differences between the two to help you decide how much hardscape and softscape you would like in your garden. Firstly, hardscape is more permanent than softscape. You can easily replace grasses, flowers, shrubs, and groundcovers, whereas installing a hardscape element should be considered a long-term decision. The advantage of the changeability of softscape is that you can easily try different garden designs by planting other shrubs, plants, and flowers from year to year. This is great because your personal style and preferences may change over time, and your garden can reflect that. Try not to change your trees, though, because the most rewarding experience comes from seeing your trees' growth.

Another difference is that softscape has the power to create a mood. Plants and nature's colour, texture, and fragrance create a calming and welcoming atmosphere.

In contrast, hardscape elements are not alive and create a sterile environment when used in isolation.

If you are struggling with generating design ideas, there are three golden rules of garden design you can use to help you. Firstly, consider movement. Avoid having straight paths that cut the garden in half; meandering pathways always create mystery and interest by hiding and revealing particular views. Secondly, place your plants away from the edges and boundaries of your yard. Bringing them into central areas naturally breaks the garden into separate spaces and guides the eye through the garden. The third golden rule is to have a destination point. It can be as simple as having two seats to enjoy the views and fragrances of your garden. A destination point will prevent you from returning inside after a minute or two. It will allow you to relax and appreciate your garden.

2
How To Avoid Disastrous Design

Your garden is not just a piece of land extending from your house. Instead, it is a sacred space that can heal you if done correctly, so getting the design of your garden right is crucial for many reasons. To give you some perspective, here are some thoughts from some of the most influential people in the field of garden design:

> ***Monty Don - Gardener, Writer, and TV Presenter***: "when you are sad, a garden comforts. When you are [humiliated, a garden consoles]. When you are consumed by anxiety, it will soothe you, and when the world is a dark and bleak place, it shines a light to guide you on."

James Wong - botanist, broadcaster, and science writer: "as a plant scientist and home gardener, I am a passionate believer in the therapeutic power of plants."

Ellen Mary - gardener, writer, and presenter: "When I spend time outside, I instinctively feel a natural shift allowing me to tune in with everything around - from birdsong, worms working the soil, and watching plants bloom, to the changing seasons. [It's about remembering that we *are* nature]. This mindful process is so good for our well-being. [Gardening allows you to view the world in a whole new way every day.]."

***

Now that we know how vital a garden can be to our well-being and overall happiness let's ensure yours is everything you have ever wanted. To begin, let's look at common garden design mistakes so that you are fully aware of what they are and how to avoid them.

Firstly, remember your front yard (if you have one). Your front yard directly affects the appeal of your home, as guests, neighbours, and potential buyers form a first impression of the first part of the property they see. It is also an indicator of what the inside of your home may look like, so if your front yard is inviting and well-designed, the rest of your property is most likely to follow suit.

Secondly, you want to ensure you set a budget for your project in advance. Landscaping your backyard into a sensational place doesn't have to cost an arm and a leg. Still, you need to set aside a certain amount of money to know what design ideas are realistic and achievable for you. If you do this, creating your dream garden will be a lot easier and freeing because you will know from the beginning what you can afford to include (allowing your imagination to go wild with possibilities within your budget). If you don't set a budget, you may end up in unexpected debt or will most likely spend much more than you initially thought you would. You might even have to halt your project halfway because you run out of money.

Thirdly, always consider the maintenance that comes with your design elements; a native plant selection is a wonderful choice for those who want little maintenance.

It means you will need to water them much less than exotic plants. On the other hand, non-native species will need more care to make them thrive, as they are not in their natural environment or climate. Another example is having a natural vs artificial lawn; the former will require mowing, weeding, fertilising, and aerating. It will also need thousands of gallons of water over time and the equipment to perform all these tasks. It is, therefore, a drain on your time, money, and water (which sounds entirely unsustainable to me). Whereas an artificial lawn requires no maintenance, it must be cleaned and fluffed occasionally.

Fourthly, when designing multiple outdoor areas, ensure you take a holistic approach. By this, I mean looking at your property from all angles and creating a cohesive design. Ideally, one place should flow into the next, and you want to make each space work together visually and functionally. You can do this by considering and implementing the landscape design principles we learned about earlier into your front, side, and backyards.

Fifthly, remember who is going to be using the yard. Is it just you and your family or guests and perhaps pets too? To simplify this, make two lists: first, list how you currently use your yard. Then, make a list of how you want to use your yard, remembering to consider the needs of all potential users.

Another soul-crushing design mistake is forgetting to plan for irrigation. Watering by hand is wasteful in water and time, so you must install an irrigation system and have this in your design plan. If you don't, extra costs will incur, and your new landscaping will likely be ruined after having to be dug up. You also need to consider how to control the amount of irrigation for each zone in your garden; overwatering any plant wastes water and money, so ensure you set a timer for the highest efficiency. If you make the right choices in the design phase, you will spend less time on maintenance and more time on enjoyment in the garden.

The next design mistake people often make is not adapting to their climate. For example, Southern California experiences heavy rainfall from time to time due to the length of the dry season experienced there. Resultantly, many Southern Californian homes have a drainage swale to cope with the level of rain and reduce to risk of flooding and erosion. Suppose your garden is susceptible to erosion in any area. In that case, it is vital to incorporate an erosion prevention strategy such as this one. The consequences can be severe if you don't, including a home-damaging mudslide. You can plan for erosion by building a retaining wall, grading your garden, or having plants on a hillside. You can also use erosion control grids, construct basins around trees and shrubs, and choose deep-rooted groundcovers (which is the easiest solution).

The eighth mistake is not designing any areas for privacy in your backyard; you may have a lovely spa installed but realise you can't enjoy it without the prying eyes of the neighbours. It is, therefore, essential to plan for private areas during the design phase so you can pick the best design strategies to control views and reduce noise. One example of backyard privacy is planting screening trees along a garden boundary. For sound, consider including a fountain for the relaxing sound of running water to drown out outside noise while making it hard for others to hear your conversations. You can install a privacy screen or shade sail for a more overt option.

The ninth mistake is forgetting to consider local biodiversity. It is better for both parties to include wildlife in your design strategy because destroying habitats for human enjoyment is the opposite of how we should live. We live in an ever-changing climate, and the last thing we need to do is create landscapes that are a detriment to the environment that don't function sustainably. To accommodate wildlife, you first need to know your local biodiversity. For example, if your area has deer, you may not want to hinder their natural movement patterns. So, consider using fences that are low enough for them to jump over and pass through. If that idea horrifies you and you want to keep deer out, use an unjumpable fence to protect any growing fruit or veg from being eaten. (Tip: to soften the look of a fence, you can plant climbers along it for added appeal, such as 'American Beauty'). You can also decide which animals or insects you would like to attract and repel. For instance, you may want bees, butterflies, and hummingbirds but not rabbits in your garden. It is best to research what animals and insects frequent your area before deciding on planting and strategies.

Number ten is failing to consider trees and how they affect your garden now and in the future. Remember to check your chosen tree species' full height and spread before planting it in your yard; otherwise, your nearby hardscape elements may be badly affected. For instance, a tree with expansive roots planted too closely to your home or driveway will result in structural damage. (Another widespread mistake is that people plant their trees too deeply when they only require the depth of the root ball.) You might even plant a small tree that frames your garden view nicely presently but will obscure your view in a few years. Likewise, check your trees' canopy cover. More coverage will hide the night sky (which is problematic if you like stargazing), despite its capacity to provide shade during the day. To avoid all of these issues, include your tree in your design plan at the maximum spread (and note down the height) so that you can plan around it. Then, once you know its maximum growth capacity, you can place it in the most convenient area for you.

The eleventh mistake is not having a large enough patio. If you are a social butterfly, the chances are that you will be spending the majority of your garden time with others, entertaining guests, and having family cookouts. Therefore, you should make your patio as large as possible for your yard size (remembering other landscaping elements you want to include). An excellent minimum patio size is ten by ten feet, as it still accommodates people spaciously while allowing for a seating area. However, only do this if you have limited space, as a more extensive patio will always be better for hosting.

Another mistake that makes designers weep inside is not creating a colour palette before building your new garden. An aesthetically pleasing garden has good placement of features, concealed views, and well-planned colour. Whether this means choosing flowers that complement your home or painting your hardscape a specific colour to match the rest of the garden theme, creating a colour palette is a must. If you don't, your garden will look amateur and poorly designed, no matter how well-placed everything may be. You could have too many colours, which ultimately reduces the appeal of your overall design, or you could end up with a garden lacking any interest or personality. You might even choose colours that don't work well together, equalling a total garden DISASTER. Luckily, you can prevent this altogether by examining the colour wheel and picking a scheme based on your favourite colour (during the design phase). For example, if your favourite colour is blue, you could choose an analogous colour scheme which is blue-based; a monochromatic colour scheme using various hues of blue; or a complementary scheme, combining shades of blue with shades of orange.

The next problem to note is having an overcrowded yard. Keep any non-functional ornaments to a minimum when designing your garden to avoid clutter. It is possible to have too many trees, statutes, and ornaments; it can make your garden look disorganised and messy. It is also unfavourable to the nature you choose to plant; trees, plants, and shrubs all need sufficient space to grow and thrive. Limiting their growing space will only harm their flourishing and your overall design. Always consider their size when they reach full maturity when planning the planting. Generally, keep your garden simple and clean as it is easier to maintain and looks better aesthetically.

***

Lighting is vital in a garden, especially for those who want to entertain. Having an outdoor lighting plan is imperative for safety reasons. It also gives your yard added visual appeal at night. (That doesn't mean I encourage you to turn the outdoor lighting on even when you're not using the garden just because it looks better; that would be highly wasteful and unsustainable). Lighting will keep people in the designated walking areas instead of accidentally trampling on your beautiful flowerbeds. It can also set the mood for evening entertainment and give you time to extend your cookout. When chosen and placed carefully, lighting can also highlight the focal points in your garden. If you don't include outdoor lighting in your design plan, you will have to incorporate it afterwards, which can be highly inconvenient. The most practical spaces may already be in use by new plants, trees, flowerbeds, or hardscapes.

Let's delve a little deeper into outdoor lighting. Most homeowners desire multi-purpose lighting (lighting that has more than just one function). For example, lighting for safety purposes can also be used as task illumination. This lighting type is installed in commonly used garden areas like the patio or deck. Another function of lighting is aesthetics, which depends on your style and what you want to achieve in your garden. To choose, consider which garden features you want to bathe in light. For example, you may want to have a string of lights dotted along the perimeter of your garden for a magical effect. Or highlight some of your favourite garden features, such as a fountain or tree, using targeted illumination.

There are many types of outdoor lighting to consider. Firstly, solar lights. You can purchase almost all outdoor lights in solar models. These use the sun to charge during the day so that the energy can be used to illuminate your garden at night. Secondly, path lights are literally lights placed along pathways, driveways, and other ground surfaces. These are great at lighting the way for people to know where they are going and at showcasing softscape features such as plants, flowers, and trees. You can also highlight hardscape features using small spotlights; architectural features can suddenly look dramatic, lit from below. Thirdly, backlights are positioned behind garden elements to create silhouettes and auras, resulting in a glowing effect. Good backlight positions are usually behind statues and shrubs. Uplights are used to make focal points by highlighting certain garden elements. They point upwards, being situated at ground level. Downlights are the opposite - placed from above to shine light downwards. They are great for imitating natural light and are usually used for security. Deck/step lights are used to illuminate steps and railings on decks, as well as being used to provide light on walkways. Wall lights are in various styles, from floodlights to front door lights. Accent lights include string lights, post lights, underwater lights, and torches. Their primary purpose is to create an atmosphere.

Now that we know the main types of lighting, you are well-equipped to begin considering which lighting type suits you. Just ensure that the range of lights you choose all work cohesively in your design.

***

People sometimes believe that the home and the garden are not connected. When designing your garden and planting plan, you must consider which plants will work with the style of your home; some plants work nicely with specific styles of architecture, while others do not. Mismatching elements are not limited to softscape though - many hardscape materials only match certain architectural styles too. For example, if you have a Mediterranean-style home, you should not use a brick driveway, but one paved with stone would look ideally in place. Consider how your garden would look from within your home. For instance, if you are fortunate enough to have a fantastic view of mountains beyond your backyard, you should avoid blocking that view by planting a screening tree there. If you like sitting outside to eat (like me), ensure the view from that spot is pleasant.

One mistake that people can be victims of is impulse buying. If the item is outside your budget or purchasing plan, don't buy it; if you don't have this discipline, you may spend a lot more than you originally wanted to, resulting in potential debt and an overcrowded garden. However, suppose you fall in love with a feature you hadn't planned for and realise your new garden will be rubbish without it. In that case, you can buy it (providing you properly research it and ensure that it does add value to your yard before doing so). Before purchasing any unplanned elements, you must consider whether it fits into the overall design and aesthetic, how they will work with your irrigation zones and lighting plans; and if the cost of this new feature will mean removing something else from your purchasing plan.

Another mistake many newbie garden designers make is adhering to straight lines for everything. Although straight lines are used in formal gardens and are great for creating symmetry, be mindful of overusing them. They may make your garden look uninviting and lack feeling. A well-balanced design has a mixture of line types; even if you favour straight lines and the clean-cut look, it's best to include some meandering, curved lines to add a sense of mystery and visual appeal. Curved lines will also give your garden a soft, natural look, rather than manufactured and industrial.

One HUGE mistake you want to avoid is not considering fire safety, especially if you live in a climate susceptible to droughts. Some measures include maintaining and reducing weeds, storing firewood far away from hardscape elements, and choosing fire-resistant plants (more on this in Chapter 4). If you do not take these precautions, you may suffer from losing your home, possessions, and possibly even life. Yes, that sounds dramatic, but it's the truth. So, take extra precautions, folks, especially concerning something as unpredictable as nature.

Regarding safety, remember to include home security in your landscape design since it directly impacts how safe you and your family are. There are many ways to make your garden design safer. However, some methods are so simple you'll wonder how it is even considered a safety feature.

Increasing your home security doesn't necessarily mean installing CCTV cameras in your yard. You could make easy design decisions and simple switches, like choosing a gravel pathway over a stone path so that you can hear when people approach your property. Another simple decision is to ensure that would-be dark corners are illuminated to prevent anyone from sneaking around your home. Lighting and motion-sensitive lights are clever ways to know when someone is near your house and is a great way to reduce the likelihood of being burgled. Trimming your hedges is another covert method to keeping thieves at bay, as it removes the potential for someone to hide behind them conveniently. Three feet is a good maximum height for hedges, so your yard is not entirely cut off from your neighbourhood. You can still have privacy with well-trimmed hedges, but make sure you arrange them in a way that lets you see behind them. You can also use thorny bushes to restrict neighbours' views while preventing anyone from hiding. Another tip is to use straight lines in your front yard from the street leading up to your house, mainly just for a clear line of sight. Maintenance should also not be underestimated; well-looked-after gardens indicate that the property is being lived in and is, therefore, much less likely to be broken into. If you are away from your property often, consider hiring a maintenance person to keep everything looking top-notch.

The next mistake is choosing the wrong plants for your climate and garden microclimate (which refers to the specific conditions created by the elements in your garden). Before making a planting plan, you must make a list of plants you want to include in your garden. Then, you should research each plant's maximum height, spread, and growing conditions to know what to expect and how to care for them. Knowing this is vital to keeping your yard looking clean and well-designed; if you don't bother with the background reading, you may end up with plants that conceal a view you were trying to create or plants that constantly die because they can't grow in your garden's microclimate. It is also necessary to know how each plant you choose will behave and look each season to avoid unwanted deadheads. A good starting point is selecting from a list of native plants since they naturally grow in your region. Natives also save water and time as they don't need much maintenance to flourish. You also need to place plants strategically in your garden to be grouped by their specific light, watering, and soil needs. This will help you plan your irrigation zones.

Let's talk about pets. If you have a pet using your garden as a restroom, you must incorporate this into your landscape plan. Consider whether you want to design a particular area just for your pet to do its business or prefer a more subtle approach. A practical solution to this is to use artificial turf, as it won't go brown or have a build-up of bacteria like natural grass would after being used as a loo for an extended period. You can easily clean artificial grass too.

The next mistake is completely disregarding any existing landscape features in your garden. Although some yards may need a complete makeover, yours might have features still good enough to use as part of your new garden. Even if the existing features are not in the correct place for your new garden vision, consider moving them somewhere else within the garden. This way, you save money by reducing your spending on new features. Reusing and repurposing garden elements is also a sustainable choice because it uses less energy and creates no pollution.

Additionally, repurposing items can be highly gratifying; it gets the creative juices flowing as you find ways to incorporate garden elements that already add value to your garden into your new landscape design. Examples of features you could reuse include boulders and trees; boulders are typically pricey, so reusing ones you may already have is a fantastic money-saving idea. Trees can be trimmed and cleaned to look tidy and presentable for your new yard. Using existing elements in your garden can save you loads of time. It may even be a source of inspiration for your new garden design.

This next mistake could make or break your garden design outcome. It could be the difference between your dream and your nightmare. Suppose your dream garden means more than just replanting a few flowers, picking a new tree, and rearranging some garden elements. In that case, you may want to hire a landscaping professional. Although this can be costly, a landscape architect will design a plan for your new garden, incorporating all the elements you wish for. Hiring a professional can ultimately save you time and money and ensures that the outcome of your garden is exactly what you envisioned. They also help you understand and discover your personal landscaping needs. This is recommended if you are making a wholly new landscape.

3
Brilliant Beginnings: Getting Going

Now that we know everything you should avoid let's move on to getting started.

The most important thing you can do to begin your design is to put a design plan together on paper. This vital step will not only save you precious time and money, but it will also be much likelier to result in a garden that you love. The design process considers many factors, including the environmental conditions of your garden, your garden needs and wants, and the all-important principles of landscape design we learned about earlier. Your ultimate goal is to arrange all your desired features (natural and artificial) into a beautiful, functional, and sustainable garden.

The design process has five main steps, which are: 1) completing a site analysis and inventory; 2) defining your needs; 3) making diagrams; 4) developing design plans; and 5) establishing a final design.

Step one analyses existing soil, climate conditions, drainage, and existing plants/trees. This step is imperative to inform your plant selection and location because each plant has different growing requirements. Similarly, the same conditions also affect you and your design decisions; if you conclude that your garden gets plenty of sunlight, you may decide to add shade cover for relaxation and give your plants a chance to thrive under the right conditions.

Step two is to make a physical list of everything you ever wanted in your dream garden. Seeing these items and ideas written down helps immensely inform your overall design plan. Doing these first two steps of the design process also aids in choosing a theme and style for your new garden. Next, you can plan where you want certain elements to go from your list. Then, you can locate spaces of activity (where people will use the site) and use this information to form a conceptual plan. Lastly, a final design plan is made, including all the softscape and hardscape details you originally had on your list. Throughout this entire five-step process, there are ten essential factors to remember:

> Know your site for selecting plants and locating activities.

Be mindful of the user(s) by considering your garden desires and needs.

Form a theme and develop your style to organise your landscape elements and dictate colour and form choices.

Create landscape 'rooms' by classifying areas of activity and finding ways to link elements together.

Consider what you want to achieve with your plant selection for the user and the environment.

Use massing and layering techniques to arrange your planting.

Create focal points and areas of transition.

Be attentive when selecting colours, textures, and materials.

Consider the factor of time when choosing plants and tree species.

Make environmentally friendly decisions by using sustainable design practices.

We will now go into detail for each of these points.

A thorough site analysis is critical in influencing your plant selection because it informs you of your current environmental conditions, letting you know what you can and cannot successfully grow. You will need to determine the soil type, topography (which refers to the physical features of the ground surface), and regional climate. Different soil types have different nutrient and moisture retention properties. Therefore, you can use your soil type to determine which plants will thrive in your garden. Although it is possible to change your soil type, it is not recommended because it is an added cost and is usually unsuccessful. To find out your soil type, you can use the existing plants in your garden to provide clues. Do this by noting where the successful plants grow and their soil conditions. You can then use this to inform your plant selection by choosing plants with similar growth requirements. You should also note down where your existing plants are not thriving so that you can make adjustments for your new plants. Remember that different plant species have their own drainage needs, and topographical conditions influence your site's drainage. If you notice that your existing drainage is poor, analysing it allows you to decide where to make adjustments. Your new garden should direct water into other landscape areas, away from your home.

Knowing your climate and garden microclimate is vitally important; you must know your site's highest and lowest temperatures to choose plants that can cope and thrive in these temperatures. The USDA Plant Hardiness Zone Map is a great resource to help you select appropriate plants for your zone. However, your yard may have specific microclimates that will change the growing conditions slightly; for instance, if you have a large tree that casts shade, you have an area of the yard that requires shade-tolerant plants. This is why drawing an existing plan for your site is critical to understanding the current microclimate conditions. Plants generally have four categories in which they can be classified: full sun, full shade, partial sun, and partial shade. You also need to note the manufactured existing conditions, such as power lines, roof overhangs, and underground utilities (as these factors also determine plant location). Measuring your existing hardscape structures correctly by using a surveyor's plat to see the boundaries you are working within is essential. Not doing so can be a huge mistake.

When I say user, I mean people/creatures using the site, including you, your family, guests, pets, and local wildlife. Each user has their own specific needs, so here are five questions to be mindful of:

Currently, how do you use the garden?

How would you like to use the garden?

How would you like your dream garden to look?

What level of maintenance are you prepared to put in?

What is your budget?

By acknowledging how you currently use your garden, you can designate spaces in your new garden to accommodate these uses (if you want to continue using your garden that way). The budget should include the cost of maintenance, installation, and materials. Be realistic about maintaining your garden; consider how much time and money you can spend on it. Asking yourself these essential questions will help you choose features and create a design most suitable for you and your lifestyle.

Picking a theme for your design is not only helpful in creating a well-put-together look; it also helps to determine your softscape and hardscape. When gathering inspiration from books, magazines, neighbouring gardens, and other sources, critically examine the garden features and layout to amass ideas you can adapt to your dedication, budget, and site. Although before deciding on a theme, consider your property's surroundings - then you can choose how you would like to control the views. For instance, consider if you want to create a garden enclosure by blocking views and linking it to your property alone or if you would rather connect your garden to its surroundings by opening up views. Views you choose to have can frame your theme.

When starting to compile a theme, consider the following factors: the architectural style of your house; your neighbourhood; the topography of your yard; and the types of landscapes found in your region. These factors will affect your choices and, if appropriately considered, will ensure that your yard fits in with the surroundings. There are two types of themes: form and style. They differ because all gardens need a form theme, but only some have a style theme. Most residential gardens use the same materials, colours, and forms as the house. Form themes ascertain the layout of space, how elements are organised in the yard, and the links between them. Therefore, form themes help produce activity spaces. Examples of form themes include geometric (circle, rectangle, square), naturalistic (with organic edges) or meandering lines. You can combine form themes with geometric forms in hardscapes and natural forms in softscape.

Style themes, on the other hand, are often related to architecture. Themes can represent many things, including a time period, a feeling, a culture, a place, or architecture. Traditional themes can be trusted as they have been used historically, so elements are guaranteed to work well together. Formal and informal landscapes are often determined by the architectural styles that the landscape is for. You can get inspired by France, Spain, Italy, and the Middle East for formal garden design. Alternatively, look to England, America and Oriental countries to inspire a more informal style. You can also apply style themes to your planting plan; depending on your theme, you may choose between woodland, meadow, tropical, desert, marsh, or coastal plant groupings. How you arrange them depends on your aesthetic desire; you may want to choose a selection for their colour, form, or texture.

***

You can contemplate your yard as having three main areas: one area to invite guests into your home; another area for entertaining, relaxing, and playing; and another area for functionality, such as growing vegetables, making compost, or working outside. These are typically the front, back, and side yards, respectively. A successful design will create separated yet linked spaces, usually through screening, garden walls, a change in paving and levels, and structures such as arbours. You should place and use garden features carefully to define your garden rooms. To get started, use the outer wall of your house as part of one defining garden room. Try to link spaces of the same activity, such as cooking and eating. An example of rooms you may want separate is a play area and a relaxation area. To achieve continuity, consider using the same or similar materials in the garden hardscape to the home.

You can also think about organising and linking spaces by considering pedestrian circulation in your garden. For example, outdoor rooms are usually connected through pathways and steps. Visual features can also link spaces together, such as using consistent planting and hardscape materials or textures. You can direct the movement of people by having certain garden elements that stand out from the rest, such as focal points. These will grab the user's attention and give them a destination. You should aim to create a wondrous garden experience by guiding the user through different rooms with different ambiences.

Plants also adhere to the rule of three with three main landscape functions. These are:

1. **Aesthetics**: plants have the power to enhance an environment's characteristics and feel. They make a place nicer to be in and simultaneously organise spaces.

2. **Serviceable**: plants help control light, humidity,

and temperature conditions (e.g. a tree's canopy providing shade). They can also be fragrant and have noise-reducing qualities, as well as being able to grow food for both people and wildlife. Certain plants can be used for screening and privacy, and you can achieve different levels of privacy depending on the plant. For example, hedges are overt barrier styles since they are tall, usually blocking views and access. In contrast, you could choose a selection of low-growing plants to block access while providing a view. Plants are also great at erosion control, retaining soil moisture, regulating organic matter, and purifying the air. Therefore, plant selections should be made at the early planning stages (after site analysis); their many capabilities and functions will help you define your outdoor rooms.

3. **Structure**: large pieces of vegetation, such as trees and some shrubs, are very influential in the design of your garden. This is because they heavily affect the placement of other garden elements and contribute heavily to home security and your yard's microclimates. You can think of plants

as nature's walls; shrubs can be seen as walls, while tree canopies can be seen as ceilings. Plants should be structured strategically (using massing and layering) to achieve particular effects, such as enclosure. Each plant mass depends on the yard's total size and each plant's size. It is also dependent on the effect you are aiming for. For instance, to connect plants in a pattern, you may want to layer them horizontally and vertically so that each plant mass is next to, in front of, or behind another. Repeating and having similar plant masses throughout a garden is a great way to create a cohesive garden design. An important factor to consider when massing plants are each plant's characteristics; the plants next to each other should complement or contrast one another. Plant compositions usually start with larger structures, such as trees and shrubs. Larger structures can control the size of the space and frame and separate areas. These larger plants are often followed by midground and low-growing plants. The latter often become focal points.

You can use unique plants, ornaments, and structures to accentuate important points in your yard. For example, you may highlight entrances to different garden rooms using steps, gates, arbours, or colourful plants. You can determine the salient points of your garden by looking at your garden style and theme; some themes have distinct elements typical of that specific garden style. An example of this is having a central water feature, which is typical of Islamic gardens.

***

You can add detail to the landscape via the visual quality of plants and hardscape. Sensory experiences such as sound, smell, and touch also add detail to the landscape. The fragrance of plants; the sound of trickling water from a fountain; the feel of the breeze as it caresses the tree canopy; and the colours of the garden hardscape are all part of the garden experience. Light's effect on plants is a detail often overlooked; the way that the sun shines on a piece of vegetation can change its appearance. For example, the sun's beams through feathery grass can make it look glowing.

By combining form, colour, texture, and size in several ways, you can enhance the visual quality of your garden. Form is often the most important characteristic of a plant when considering its aesthetic value in your garden, followed by texture. However, plant colour sometimes dominates the garden's look at certain times during the year. One way of maximising plant colour throughout the year is by choosing plants with colour in their bark, foliage, and fruit.

It is important to remember that your garden is, after all, influenced by nature, and its appearance and functions will change throughout the day and year.

After analysing your site, you are ready to make a plant list. Three factors should inform your decision for each plant: 1) its rate of growth, 2) the maintenance it needs, and 3) its maximum height and spread.

Consider its growth rate because you may not want some plants to be fully grown while others are still maturing; this could spoil your design intent and ruin the garden's look. You should, of course, consider the maintenance each plant needs to keep your garden looking superb without resenting the effort you must put into it. Lastly, knowing each plant's height and spread will help you decide where to plant it, ensuring it has enough space to thrive and doesn't interfere with your utilities and hardscape (or limit the growth of other plants by invading their space). In addition, if plants are grown too close together, maintenance is even more challenging.

***

Let's briefly talk about sustainability in the garden. To create a sustainable garden, you can do many things, but a great starting point is to choose resource-efficient plants, control your water usage (by installing irrigation zones and recycling water for fountains), and buy hardscape structures that have been made from recycled, reused, upcycled, or locally sourced materials. Another way to be environmentally conscious is to consider your existing garden and decide what elements (both softscape and hardscape) you can keep. Some existing plants might need to be moved elsewhere in your garden to fit into your new design and grow more effectively. It is also helpful to start making a plant list of plants native to your region.

A good trick to try is the coin trick; this will tell you if you need to replace your plant or if it is still in good health. Use your coin to scratch a tiny area of bark on a branch; if it is green or white, it is in perfect health, whereas a brown reveal means it is dead.

To be more sustainable, try to collect rainwater in your garden. During the stages of design is the best time to consider this. We are living through a global water crisis, so in the future, we will definitely face a higher degree of water scarcity (especially for those living in drought-prone climates). Therefore, we must treat the water used in the garden with respect and care. Using a rainwater harvesting system to collect, direct, and store water for irrigation should be a priority in your garden design plan. If you plan this early enough in the process, it can add aesthetic value to your garden. Installing a rainwater catchment system involves some earthworks and underground pipework, so it is usually installed first.

Choosing a sustainable hardscape is not rocket science. It just means finding ones that use materials with non-toxic chemicals. It also means taking any opportunity to reuse any existing hardscape parts you own to make new ones. Reusing elements is both budget-friendly and eco-friendly as it reduces the need to buy completely new hardscapes and the amount of waste sent to landfills. Suppose you do not have any current hardscape but are looking to reuse and repurpose hardscape material. In that case, you can look to your local community.

You can do a few more things to ensure you are designing in the most sustainable way. Firstly, do not make changes that will directly harm the environment or your local biodiversity when planning to re-landscape. Secondly, consider if any of the work you must undertake will cause damage to humans and the environment; if so, be open to alternative solutions. Furthermore, when ordering new hardscape and planting new softscape, aim to choose locally sourced materials and native plant selections to reduce transportation costs and emissions.

Thirdly, design your garden with nature in mind; it is always better to go with nature than against it. This means considering your regional climate (by choosing plants that require the least irrigation) and considering how to best make the most of the rainfall by collecting rainwater or turning your runoff into a stream. You could also make a natural windbreak if you live in a windy climate using evergreen shrubs and trees. A windbreak will protect you and your property from the wind and lower the need for heating your home, saving you money. Similarly, you could plant deciduous species to provide shade and reduce your air conditioning bills in the summer.

Fourthly, you should protect and conserve existing habitats in your garden and plan your design around that to not disturb nature. To go the extra mile, you could design your garden to actively support ecosystem services, for example, by planting pollinator plants.

Fifthly, when using tools to maintain your garden, pick the renewably sourced ones, such as solar-powered or electric, over gas-powered tools since the latter can be greatly pollutive and inefficient. You can also create compost from fallen leaves and vegetation trimmings, reducing waste and removing the need for importing products for good soil health.

We will go more in-depth about sustainable garden design in a later chapter.

***

Analysing site conditions

Now that we are well-versed in things to consider, let's look at what a site analysis and inventory really mean.

A site inventory considers any existing condition affecting people, plants, and water. You can inform your decisions about plant placement, activity areas, and managing rainwater based on the information you collect on these three factors.

On the other hand, a site analysis is a conclusion you make based on the current list of conditions you have identified using your site inventory. In other words, you use your site inventory to conduct site analysis. Your site analysis should also involve a plan of action to fix any existing landscaping problems you may have.

Making a site inventory is easier than it sounds. All you really need to do is walk around your yard and note down (on paper) all that you see and feel. Be mindful of what works and doesn't work from an aesthetic and functional point of view. Then consider what is worth saving and what should change, considering soil conditions, plants, sun patterns, hardscape, views, topography, and activity areas.

Knowing your soil type is vital before picking your plant selection. Each plant has different drainage requirements. Examining your existing vegetation can also test your soil for any issues.

Then you must know what climate conditions you are working with so that you can pick the best plants and hardscape finishes to suit your garden. Microclimate areas within your garden often include the sunniest and shadiest areas. You can define sunny areas as ones that receive six or more hours of sunlight per day and shady areas as ones that are in full shade for the same time frame. However, remember that seasonality affects sun and shade patterns, and growing softscape such as trees and shrubs may also begin to cast shade later on. Your garden's aspect (north, east, south, or west) also determines how much sun and shade you receive. It would help if you also considered wind, as it can make plants dry and carry sea salt in coastal areas.

Noting down your existing hardscape is necessary for a site inventory because they influence where your new plant beds and hardscape will go. A surveyor's plat will help you define the boundaries and dimensions of your property so that you can plan your new garden accordingly. Also, note down the materials your property currently uses and their style, as it may inform design decisions you make later on. If you do not have a plat, ensure you hire a surveyor.

With development codes, people desire to fit in with their neighbourhood. By adding aesthetic value to the local area, we are judged more positively by our neighbours. Be mindful of the neighbourhood's architectural style, vegetation types, and the general character of the area as a starting point to fitting in. You may notice that many local gardens have similar features, and this may be due to design codes that they must adhere to. Usually, the codes restrict fencing, furniture, and ornaments while providing a list of plant recommendations.

As we discussed before, the main aim of site analysis is to create a list of actions informed by your site inventory. These actions should fix existing problems you may have as well as give you ideas of where to locate new design features. For example, you may analyse your current drainage conditions and find that you must redirect rainwater away from your home. Simultaneously, you can plan to design a rainwater catchment system. You may analyse the viewpoints in your yard and decide you would like more privacy. You also may have a dream plant list, but some do not work with your current site conditions. Your action plan from your site analysis will help you rearrange features in your yard to accommodate your dream plants (i.e. by creating more shade or exposing more of your site to the sun). Of course, you will also immediately notice which vegetation you want to keep and which you wish to eliminate. Most yards have places that often need special attention; these include sensitive areas that should be protected (such as mini wildlife habitat or an eco-corridor where your local wildlife currently passes through). You can also note down less severe things like areas for a potential focal point or splash of colour. Since the analysis provides actions, you should write it as a list of instructions for you to follow as part of the design process. Remember that nothing has been set in stone at this stage and that the proposed locations of your new garden elements can change.

***

Will my design work for my yard?

The first question to ask yourself is if your design includes materials from the surrounding architecture. If so, you are on the right track because a design that shares materiality with the existing surroundings will likely fit in and look "in place". Next, check your colour palette against your house and see if you have picked a colour scheme using the colour wheel or whether you do not have a well-thought-out scheme. If the latter is true, begin thinking of alternatives to achieve your desired look while making your design well-rounded.

Secondly, examine your house's outline in relation to your yard size with the proper measurements written down. From this, you can determine if you have space for all the landscaping features you originally wanted. You will also be able to see the shapes of your property from above, helping you to decide on forms that will work well within your landscape. For example, you may notice that your existing garden plan uses many straight lines; therefore, to make a well-balanced design, you should plan to add some naturalistic lines. The shape of your home can also indicate what shapes may work well in the garden; for instance, if your house uses hexagonal shapes, a hexagonal form could look nice in your yard.

Thirdly, there are typical garden design layouts you can measure yours against to see if it works. Usually, the most-used features are placed close to the entrance to the garden for ease of access. For example, patios are typically adjacent to people's homes for comfort. Functional features, such as a vegetable patch, are located on the side (hidden from view), while play areas are situated in front of the kitchen for parents to keep an eye on their children.

You may use texture and colour to distinguish between your garden rooms by adding visual weight to areas of importance. A good design should have some form of visual hierarchy. For example, having an outdoor space of a different size to all other garden rooms indicates its difference and thus importance.

You can also test the success of your outdoor design by evaluating the movement patterns within your new landscape plan. For example, suppose spaces are connected visually and physically through pathways, focal points, and the careful use of materials. In that case, you are likely to have a good design plan.

4
A Climate-Conscious Garden

As you now know, you must know your garden inside-out before beginning to plan a successful garden design. If you have noticed that you live in a regional climate with wildly fluctuating temperatures and weather conditions, this chapter will help immensely. Yes, some plants can withstand even the most hostile conditions, such as drought, wind, cold, and severe rainfall.

<u>Xeriscaping</u>

First, let's look at drought-tolerant landscaping. The term simply means growing plants that thrive in climates with little rainfall. Most drought-tolerant plants are native to the region in that they are grown. However, drought-resistant plants differ slightly because they can live through long periods without watering. In other words, you can describe plants adapted to arid climates as drought-tolerant or drought resistant. Another common term for this landscaping style is xeriscaping, a landscape that uses drought-tolerant plants.

There are many positives to xeriscaping. In regions that experience seasonal droughts, such as Texas, Georgia, California, and Australia, conserving water using a plant selection that doesn't require watering makes sense. Xeriscaping is especially useful as these regions have incentives encouraging conserving water through water-smart landscaping.

Some xeriscaping features you can include are drought-tolerant groundcovers (such as white clover or creeping thyme); collecting and conserving rainwater; mulching beds (as this reduces evaporation); using an artificial lawn. However, if you are desperate for a natural lawn, ensure that you keep the roots healthy; if maintained properly, they can also withstand dry periods (even if they turn brown during them). To be inspired, try visiting a local garden that uses desert landscaping - you may be able to steal some ideas for your yard.

There are many benefits to xeriscaping your yard. From saving water, time, energy, and money, it's a wonder why everyone in drought-prone climates (such as San Diego and most of the Southwestern United States) isn't landscaping this way. It is a very sustainable way to live since it reduces your carbon footprint in so many ways (as mentioned above) and minimises the need for equipment powered by non-renewable energy. Xeriscaping potentially provides wildlife habitats through a native plant selection too.

If you have fewer drought-tolerant plants in your selection, ensure to water them properly by making a dish-like hole near the base of the plant and water aiming at the roots (filling the hole you just created). Watering your plants in the evening is also best to reduce evaporation. Alternatively, you could water your plants in the early morning before the scorching sun has the chance to evaporate the moisture before the soil can absorb it. You should also avoid watering on windy days because evaporation happens more rapidly. Remember, watering your plants properly once a week, under the right circumstances, is better than watering them daily under the wrong conditions.

**

It all sounds exciting, but before jumping straight in, there are a few things you should generally know. First, research how much rainfall your area gets each year so that you can choose the right plants for your climate. Then, look up native plants that are region-specific to you (so they are more likely to thrive in your garden). Next, make a list of invasive plant species to avoid. Once you have completed these, you will be ready to start planning your drought-tolerant landscape.

It is important to remember that you are ultimately in control of how much water you save by choosing the right plants and landscaping features for your garden. Saving water through your design can look very different depending on your style, preferences, and needs. So do not believe for a second that you need to plant a bunch of cacti atop gravel to have a drought-tolerant garden. You can even have your water feature and tropical plants if you desire, but be smart about the location of these features. This means establishing different irrigation zones (as discussed earlier), ensuring that your tropical selection gets the right amount of water, light and space to grow. You should also ensure that your water feature uses greywater (domestic wastewater that faeces have not contaminated).

Another tip for conserving water in your garden is to weed regularly because weeds compete with your established plants for light, nutrients, space, and moisture.

Other than cacti and succulent plants, here is a list of drought-tolerant species to get you started:

Common Name	Zoysia grass
Botanical Name	Zoysia spp
Family	Poaceae
Plant Type	Perennial turf grass
Mature Size	4-6 inches (height)
Sun Exposure	Full
Soil Type	Well-drained
Soil pH	Acidic, neutral
Hardiness Zones	5-10 (USDA)
Native Area	Korea

This grass is popular across southern American lawns. It can grow in a range of soils and grows best with one inch of water weekly, although it is a drought-tolerant species. It is most suited to climate temperatures over 80 degrees Fahrenheit, and there are two species to choose from: *Zoysia japonica* and *Zoysia matrella*.

Common Name	Thyme
Botanical Name	Thymus vulgaris
Family	Lamiaceae
Plant Type	Herbaceous perennial
Mature Size	6-12 inches (height and spread)
Sun Exposure	Full
Soil Type	Loamy, sandy
Soil pH	Acidic to alkaline (6-8)
Hardiness Zones	5-9 (USDA)
Native Area	Mediterranean

Thyme is a fast-growing plant that needs well-drained soil and space to thrive. They can be watered as little as once a month (depending on your climate). There are four species of thyme: *Thymus x citriodorus* 'Aureus' (Golden lemon thyme); *Thymus pseudolanuginosus* (woolly thyme); *Thymus herba-barona;* (caraway thyme), and *Thymus praecox* (creeping thyme). Often, thyme is used as a groundcover; you can even create a thyme lawn.

Common Name	Lavendar
Botanical Name	Lavandula spp.
Family	Lamiaceae
Plant Type	Herbaceous perennial
Mature Size	24-36 inches (height) 24-48 inches (spread)
Sun Exposure	Full
Soil Type	Dry, well-drained
Soil pH	Alkaline
Hardiness Zones	5a-9a (USDA)
Native Area	Europe

This fragrant, calmness-stimulating plant is drought-tolerant once established but needs regular watering during its first season. Be careful not to overwater (especially in winter), as dampness kills Lavendar. Lavender has roots that spread, so be careful to give it the space it needs. Also, this plant can be toxic to cats and dogs, so if you have pets in your garden, think strategically about planting placement (or using it at all). There are four types of Lavendar: *Lavandula angustifolia* (English Lavendar); *Lavandula x intermedia* (Lavandin); *Lavandula dentata* (Fringed lavender); and *Lavendula stoechas* (French Lavendar).

Common Name	Slipper Plant, Lady Slipper
Botanical Name	Euphorbia Lomelii
Family	Lamiaceae
Plant Type	Perennial
Mature Size	36 -72 inches (height) 24-36 inches (spread)
Sun Exposure	Full
Soil Type	Sandy, well-drained
Soil pH	Alkaline, neutral, acidic
Hardiness Zones	9-11 (USA)
Native Area	Central America

This plant type is also toxic to pets, so beware. However, maintenance is very low, and they can grow in containers (which is ideal if you are low on space). Its red flowers make this plant eye-catching and attract hummingbirds (which is an added sustainable bonus). It can be watered as little as twice a month and is an excellent choice for desert landscaping.

Common Name	Aster, frost flowers
Botanical Name	Symphytrichum spp.
Family	Asteraceae
Plant Type	Herbaceous, perennial
Mature Size	12 -72 inches (height) 12- 48 inches (spread)
Sun Exposure	Full
Soil Type	Loamy, well-drained
Soil pH	Neutral, acidic
Hardiness Zones	3-8 (USDA)
Native Area	North America

Asters have expanding roots, so they need plenty of space to grow. This plant blooms daisy-like lilac flowers with yellow centres - a beautiful addition to any backyard. You should water new plants until the flowers have bloomed completely, and as a general rule, they should be watered weekly with an inch of water. A bonus of planting asters is that they can survive in frosty temperatures and last throughout the winter. Common aster species include Celeste (dark blue with yellow centres); *Aster Novi-Belgii* (Hazy - raspberry pink with yellow centres); *Callistephus Chinensis* (Puff); and *Symphyotrichum novae-angliae* (New England Aster - lavender, blue or white petals with centres that attract pollinators). The New England Aster is also a larval host to pearl crescent butterflies.

Common Name	Coreopsis, tickseed, calliopsis
Botanical Name	Coreopsis spp.
Family	Asteraceae
Plant Type	Perennial, annual
Mature Size	24 -48 inches (height) 12- 24 inches (spread)
Sun Exposure	Full
Soil Type	Sandy, well-drained
Soil pH	Neutral to acidic
Hardiness Zones	2-11 (USA)
Native Area	North America, Central America, South America

Coreopsis plants are generally relatively low maintenance when grown in their native climate. They can bloom from summer to autumn if deadheaded and should be watered regularly until they become established. Although they are drought tolerant after their first year, regular watering will make this plant thrive. There are many species of this plant, four of which are the following: *Coreopsis grandiflora* (Early Sunrise); *Coreopsis grandiflora* (Golden Showers); *Coreopsis verticillata* (Moonbeam); and *Coreopsis rosea* (Nana). The average lifetime of this plant is between three and five years, and it needs roughly six to eight hours of sunlight each day to bloom.

Common Name	Lamb's ears, Wooly Betony
Botanical Name	Stachys byzantina
Family	Lamiaceae
Plant Type	Herbaceous perennial
Mature Size	12 -18 inches (height) 12 inches (spread)
Sun Exposure	Full to partial
Soil Type	Well-drained, evenly moist to dry
Soil pH	Slightly acidic
Hardiness Zones	4a-9a (USDA)
Native Area	Middle East

This plant should be grown about 18 inches apart because they spread rapidly (but you can control this with edging). It has a fragrant, fruity smell and should have access to partial shade for the best growth in desert climates. Similar to Coreopsis plants, these drought-tolerant plants need about one inch of water weekly (when there is dry soil). It is a herbaceous species and stays evergreen in mild climates. Three of the most common cultivars of Lamb's ear are Big Ears or Helen von Stein, Silver Carpet, and Cotton Boll. Be mindful that Lamb's ear is susceptible to disease and fungal infection, so the infected leaves should be discarded, and an antifungal spray should be used. You can prevent disease and infection by ensuring the plant gets plenty of air circulation.

Common Name	Aloe Vera
Botanical Name	Aloe barbadensis miller
Family	Asphodelaceae
Plant Type	Succulent, herb, perennial
Mature Size	12-36 inches (height) 6-12 inches (spread)
Sun Exposure	Full, partial
Soil Type	Sandy
Soil pH	Acidic
Hardiness Zones	10-12 (USDA)
Native Areas	Africa

This amazing succulent has over one hundred varieties that can survive in arid climates with temperatures ranging between 60 and 75 degrees Fahrenheit. Most species need watering every other week, making it a great choice if forgetful. However, remember that some aloe species are toxic to cats and dogs. Be careful when choosing which to plant in your garden (always remember the user!). You can also use some varieties, such as Aloe Vera, as a focal point in your garden. Consider planting aloe in gravel if your regional climate experiences rain during winter, as this prevents any potential rot. Here are four types of aloe that gardeners tend to favour: *Aloe polyphylla* (spiral aloe); *Aloe aculeata*; *Aloe ciliaris* (climbing aloe); and *Aloe brevifolia* (short leaf aloe).

Common Name	Artichoke
Botanical Name	Cynara scolymus
Family	Asteraceae
Plant Type	Herbaceous, perennial, biennial
Mature Size	36-72 inches (height) 48-60 inches (spread)
Sun Exposure	Full
Soil Type	Well-drained
Soil pH	Neutral
Hardiness Zones	7-11 (USDA)
Native Areas	Mediterranean

Artichokes can be harvested for eating before the flowers develop and love to be grown under full sun. They can be ornamental and low-maintenance plants, but keep them sheltered from strong winds. They also should be watered deeply at least once or twice per week. Artichokes have several excellent species, including Big Heart; Green Globe; Imperial Star; Purple of Romagna; and Violetto. The only issues artichokes may face are slugs and aphids, but you can be rid of these fairly easily. They can also be victim to Botrytis (grey mould), which affects their flower bracts and leaves, so ensure they have good air circulation.

Common Name	Beardtongue
Botanical Name	Penstemon
Family	Plantaginaceae
Plant Type	Herbaceous, perennial
Mature Size	6-8 inches (height) 8-20 inches (spread)
Sun Exposure	Full
Soil Type	Well-drained
Soil pH	Neutral to acidic
Hardiness Zones	3-8 (USDA)
Native Areas	North America

Due to their tubular flowers, these plants are great for attracting wildlife into your garden, such as bees and hummingbirds. Beardtongue can grow in several conditions, from mountains to plains and deserts, and are drought tolerant once established. However, you should water them twice monthly if your region is experiencing a dry season. There are over 200 types of species related to this plant, so here are six common ones: Dark Towers; Elfin Pink; Husker Red; Jingle Bells (which mainly attracts hummingbirds); Pina Colada; and Red Riding Hood. Another significant fact about Beardtongue is that they are generally disease-free (if taken care of properly with correct sun and drainage needs).

Common Name	Fountain Grass
Botanical Name	Pennisetum setaceum 'Rubrum'
Family	Poaceae
Plant Type	Perennial ornamental grass
Mature Size	36-60 inches (height) 24-48 inches (spread)
Sun Exposure	Full sun, partial shade
Soil Type	Well-drained, moist
Soil pH	Neutral to acidic
Hardiness Zones	9-10 (USDA)
Native Areas	Africa, southern Asia

Fountain grass is an ornamental grass that grows in tropical climates. Therefore, they are not great at surviving in cold temperatures (20 degrees Fahrenheit is the lowest temperature they can survive in). This plant is a fantastic focal point, especially in a plant mass, as it has a vase-shaped form and is vividly coloured. Ensure to plant it sheltered from winds. Any time of the year is fine (like most ornamental grasses, though springtime is recommended). This species is fast-growing and can withstand some drought. However, as the plant is becoming established, water it once or twice a week. Three common types within this species are *Pennisetum setaceum* (Fireworks), *P. alopecuroides* (Burgundy Bunny), and *P. alopecuroides* (Little Bunny). One thing to note is that pests such as slugs and snails like to eat this ornamental grass, which needs good circulation to prevent rust fungus.

Common Name	Geranium
Botanical Name	Geranium spp.
Family	Geraniaceae
Plant Type	Herbaceous perennial
Mature Size	6-36 inches (height) 12-36 inches (spread)
Sun Exposure	Full sun, partial
Soil Type	Medium moisture, well-drained
Soil pH	Slightly acidic
Hardiness Zones	3-9 (USDA)
Native Areas	Temperate regions worldwide, Mediterranean

If you're looking for a long-lasting plant with low maintenance needs, Geraniums are for you; they can live for decades and only need watering once the soil is dry (if planted under full sun exposure, it will therefore need watering more often). There are so many geranium types that their care needs vary depending on the type you choose to plant. They grow best in climates with 65 and 75 degrees Fahrenheit during the day and 50 to 60 degrees at night. Popular choices of geranium include *Geranium Ibericum* (Johnson's Blue); *Geranium sanguineum* (Bloody Cranesbill); *Geranium himlayense* (Lilac Cranesbill); *Geranium × oxonianum* (Wargrave Pink); and *Geranium pratense* (Double Jewel). Regarding pests, slugs eat young geraniums while rust and mildew can affect foliage, so ensure to dispose of any infected leaves and allow for good circulation.

Common Name	Sweet Potato Vine
Botanical Name	Ipomea batatas
Family	Convolvulaceae
Plant Type	Herbaceous perennial
Mature Size	5-12 inches (spread)
Sun Exposure	Full sun
Soil Type	Moist, well-drained
Soil pH	Neutral to acidic
Hardiness Zones	9-11 (USDA)
Native Areas	America's tropical regions

This is a very versatile plant as it can be grown in containers, over a wall, or as a groundcover. It's worth noting that its colour will be more vibrant with more sun exposure (and will do better under sunny conditions to prevent too-wet soil from causing rot). Although this plant is drought-tolerant, keep the soil consistently moist to prevent the leaves from wilting. Four types of Sweet Potato Vine commonly used in gardens: *Ipomoea batatas* Sweet Caroline (mainly used as a groundcover); *Ipomoea batatas* Margarita or Marguerite (popularly used as a climber); *Ipomoea batatas* Blackie; and *Ipomoea batatas* Ragtime.

Common Name	Trumpet Vine, Hummingbird Vine
Botanical Name	Campsis radicans
Family	Bigononiaceae
Plant Type	Woody perennia vine
Mature Size	300-40 inches (length) 60-120 inched (width)
Sun Exposure	Full sun, partial
Soil Type	Average, moist but well-drained
Soil pH	Mildly acidic to mildly alkaline
Hardiness Zones	4-9 (USDA)
Native Areas	North America (Southeast U.S.)

This plant produces sunset-coloured flowers in summertime, attracting pollinators and hummingbirds. Grow Trumpet Vine with caution, as this plant spreads aggressively. Therefore, it is a reasonably high-maintenance plant, as you will need to ensure it doesn't invade the space of other species. However, the vine only requires minimal care to flourish; water it only when you notice wilting. They are drought-tolerant, and a climate's usual rainfall is enough for them to remain healthy. You should also note that they can be mildly toxic to humans and animals. Also, it is a highly flammable plant, so if you live in an area susceptible to wildfires, reconsider whether this is right for you. Planting it in spring or early autumn is best. There are many types of Trumpet Vine, some of which I will list: *Campus radicans* Apricot; *C. radicans* Flava; *C. radicans* Indian Summer; *C radicans* crimson Trumpet; *C. radicans* Judy; and *C radicans* Atropuppurea.

Common Name	Blue Blossom Ceanothus, Blue Mountain Lilac
Botanical Name	Ceanothus thyrsiflorus
Family	Rhamnaceae
Plant Type	Shrub
Mature Size	48-144 inches (height) 60-72 inched (width)
Sun Exposure	Full sun, partial
Soil Type	Average, moist but well-drained
Soil pH	Neutral, alkaline
Hardiness Zones	7-10 (USDA)
Native Areas	North America

Unlike many others, this shrub is relatively low-maintenance as it does not need deadheading or suffer from fungal disease. It can also withstand salt spray (from the ocean), erosion, bad-quality soil, and drought. However, young shrubs should be watered regularly for at least the first two years until well established. Ideally, you should plant it sheltered from strong winds and ensure good circulation to prevent rot (just like with all the other plants we listed above). Particularly successful uses of this shrub are on slopes and as hedges, and there are many species of this shrub. Several types include *Ceanothus thyrsiflorus* Skylark; *Ceanothus thyrsiflorus* Snow Flurry; *Ceanothus thyrsiflorus* Repens Victoria; *Ceanothus thyrsiflorus* El Dorado; and *Ceanothus thyrsiflorus* Arroyo de la Cruz.

***

Landscaping for shady and wet conditions

Now let's move on to a list of plants that thrive in the opposite conditions to drought, in case you live in this climate. It is important to note that plants will thrive in their native habitat because they are naturally adapted to those growing conditions. Therefore, the plant selection you choose should be guided by this fact to ensure the most successful garden.

Perennials

Common Name	Blue Mistflower
Botanical Name	*Conoclinium coelestinum*
Family	Asteraceae
Plant Type	Perennial
Mature Size	12-36 inches (height and spread)
Sun Exposure	Full sun, partial
Soil Type	Loamy, sandy, clay, moist
Soil pH	Neutral, mildly acidic
Hardiness Zones	5-10 (USDA)
Native Areas	Central and southeastern U.S., Canada, West Indies

These flowers are excellent pollinator attractors (bees, butterflies, and birds) and are naturally found in low woodlands, meadows, ditches, and near water sources. It can withstand freezing temperatures as its native climate experiences cold winters. Therefore, they will flourish in moist soil and be perfect for you if your microclimate constantly faces rain and cold. Blue mistflower will also grow in hot climates, but they need to be placed in partial sun only in this case (because it needs soil moisture to survive). Thus it can survive in drought periods, too, once established, as long as you consistently water the soil (about once or twice a week) to retain its moisture. However, beware that this is a quick-spreading plant that is considered an invasive species in some regions.

Common Name	Cardinal flower
Botanical Name	Lobelia cardinalis
Family	Campanulaceae
Plant Type	Herbaceous perennial
Mature Size	36-48 inches (height) 12-24 inches (spread)
Sun Exposure	Full to partial
Soil Type	Moist
Soil pH	Slightly acidic to neutral
Hardiness Zones	2-9 (USDA)
Native Areas	U.S. and Canada

The Cardinal flower is naturally found in wet areas. Maintaining soil moisture is critical as it cannot grow properly in dry soils. It helps to add mulch or compost around the plants to retain soil moisture. These requirements mean that Cardinal flowers flourish in regions with frequent rainfall. They can even withstand seasonal flooding. Planted alone, this flower lasts for a few years but can last many years in a colony. They are disease-free, but snails and slugs love foliage, so you should protect your flowers from them. If you live in a cold climate, these flowers will do best in full sunshine, and in hotter climates, it is best to plant them in the shade. You should also water it heavily twice a week if choosing to grow this in an arid climate with little rainfall. Like many plants mentioned above, Cardinal flowers need good air circulation to prevent fungal infections. There are various colours from different types of Cardinal flowers, including Queen Victoria; Black Truffle; Rosea; Alba; and Angel Song.

Common Name	New York Ironweed
Botanical Name	Vernonia noveboracensis
Family	Asteraceae
Plant Type	Herbaceous perennial
Mature Size	48-84 inches (height) 36-48 inches (spread)
Sun Exposure	Full
Soil Type	Rich, moist
Soil pH	Acidic; tolerates neutral soil
Hardiness Zones	5-9 (USDA)
Native Areas	Eastern and Southeastern North America

This native wildflower is known to be an aggressive grower and should be planted at least 24 inches apart from each other. It is also considered an invasive species, so carefully plan enough space for its planting location to protect the rest of your plant selection. This flower naturally thrives in moist soil, so it will stay alive and well if you ensure that the earth never gets dry. Therefore, if choosing to plant this in a drought-prone climate, you must water it regularly to keep the soil moist. It needs a minimum of one inch of water weekly under normal circumstances and can easily tolerate poor drainage. Other varieties of New York ironweed include *Vernonia gigantea* (Jonesboro Giant); *V. angustifolia* (Plum Peachy); *Vernonia lettermannii* (Iron Butterfly); and *Vernonia* (Summer's Surrender and Summer's Swan Song).

Ferns

Common Name	Royal Fern
Botanical Name	Osmunda regalis var. spectabilis
Family	Osmundaceae
Plant Type	Deciduous fern
Mature Size	60-72 inches (height) 12-24 inches (spread)
Sun Exposure	Full shade, partial shade, full sun
Soil Type	Moist but well-drained, poorly drained
Soil pH	Acidic, alkaline, neutral
Hardiness Zones	3-9 (USDA)
Native Areas	North America

This fern will tolerate many conditions but is particularly useful for wet areas. This fern is for you if you are looking for a low-maintenance plant. It will fit nicely into an informal-style garden in flower beds or a wildflower meadow section of your yard. It is considered medium to large for a fern and is generally disease and pest-free. It has foliage from spring until autumn, when the leaves turn a pleasant red-brown colour.

Common Name	Ground Fern, Marsh Fern
Botanical Name	Thelypteris palustris
Family	Thelypteridaceae
Plant Type	Deciduous fern
Mature Size	20-40 inches (height and spread)
Sun Exposure	Partial shade
Soil Type	Moist but well-drained, poorly drained
Soil pH	Acidic, neutral
Hardiness Zones	4-8 (USDA)
Native Areas	Eastern North America, Eurasia

Marsh fern is another option for low-maintenance gardeners; it can be planted as a groundcover or in flower borders or beds for an informal garden. It is also generally free from disease and pests and has green foliage from spring through autumn. Since it grows best in partial shade and moist soil, it will grow well in regions experiencing frequent rainfall.

Rushes

Common Name	Corkscrew Rush, Soft Rush
Botanical Name	Juncus effusus
Family	Juncaceae
Plant Type	Herbaceous perennial, evergreen
Mature Size	24-48 inches (height) 20-40 inches (spread)
Sun Exposure	Full sun to partial shade
Soil Type	Poorly drained
Soil pH	Neutral to acidic
Hardiness Zones	2-9 (USDA)
Native Areas	North and South America, Europe, Asia, Africa

You will need permanently moist soil or shallow water to grow this plant. It is an excellent choice if you live in an area prone to heavy rainfall and flooding, as it will withstand this amount of watering. Therefore, a wonderful way to incorporate Soft Rush into your design is to have them on the edges of a water feature or in containers you can sink into the water. However, beware as it spreads quickly and can be considered invasive in warmer climates if not looked after properly. The spiral-like, twisted foliage is dark green and curly, making them an interesting and focal form in the landscape. This plant is deer-resistant, so choose it to keep your yard free from deer. There are numerous varieties of Juncus effusus, four of which include: *J. effusus* Curly Wurly; *J. effusus* Big Twister; *J. effusus* Spiralis; and *J. effusus* Quartz Creek.

Shrubs

Common Name	Red Chokeberry
Botanical Name	Aronia arbutifolia
Family	Rosaceae
Plant Type	Deciduous shrub
Mature Size	72-120 inches (height) 36-72 inches (spread)
Sun Exposure	Full sun or partial shade
Soil Type	Moist, well-drained
Soil pH	Neutral to acidic
Hardiness Zones	4-9 (USDA)
Native Areas	Eastern North America

This shrub will produce fruit and flowers, providing your garden with colour and food. The flowers may be white or light pink, while the berries are a deep red (and can be made into jam). The fruit will also attract birds to the garden, especially in winter when food can be scarce. Other pollinators, such as bees and butterflies, are also attracted to the flowers produced by this shrub. This drought-tolerant shrub can withstand sea salt spray and pollution, making it an excellent choice for urban dwellers. Generally, this shrub can grow in various soil conditions but will perform best in moist soil with good drainage. The only diseases it may suffer from are twig blight and leaf spots. Still, neither is of significant concern to the plant's overall health. If you want to use this shrub as a focal point, choose the variety Brilliantissima; it will have larger fruits that stay throughout winter and more flowers and eye-catching red foliage in the autumn.

Common Name	Black Huckleberry
Botanical Name	Gaylussacia baccata
Family	Ericaceae
Plant Type	Perennial shrub
Mature Size	60 inches (height) 40 inches (spread)
Sun Exposure	Partial shade
Soil Type	Sandy, rocky
Soil pH	Acidic
Hardiness Zones	3-7 (USDA)
Native Areas	North America

Black huckleberry is a beautiful plant for seasonal interest to add to your garden. This shrub is decorated with tiny yellow or pink flowers in the spring, turning into fruit in midsummer. The autumn foliage is a stunning reddish-purple, and humans, birds, and mammals can eat their sweet berries. They naturally grow on the edges of wooded areas and in acidic forests. Once they are established, this becomes another low-maintenance plant. However, they require some watering during spring to encourage blooming and fruiting. This shrub is considered drought-tolerant but benefits from watering regularly. There are some closely related species of huckleberry, including *Vaccinium parvifolium* (red huckleberry); *Vaccinium ovatum* (evergreen huckleberry); *Vaccinium deliciosum* (blueleaf huckleberry); and *Vaccinium membranaceum* (thinleaf huckleberry).

Common Name	Summersweet, sweet pepperbush
Botanical Name	Clethra alnifolia
Family	Clethraceae
Plant Type	Deciduous shrub
Mature Size	36-96 inches (height) 48-72 inches (spread)
Sun Exposure	Full sun, partial shade
Soil Type	Loam, clay, sand
Soil pH	Acidic to neutral
Hardiness Zones	3-9 (USDA)
Native Areas	Eastern and Southern U.S.

This beautiful shrub has dense branches and is perfect for adding privacy to your garden through screens or hedges. It grows excellently in wet conditions, such as on the edges of many water features (ponds, marshes, streams), but it also looks lovely when used as part of a shrub border or in planting beds. Aim to grow this shrub in an area receiving full morning sun and afternoon shade in constantly moist soil. As Sweet Pepperbush is water-loving, it will grow well if your regional climate has heavy and frequent rainfall. Its natural habitat includes marshes, riverbanks, and swampy areas of woodland. There are a few varieties offering different flower colours and sizes, so choose according to your preference and style: Creels Calico (dark green leaves dotted with white);

Crystalina (with white flowers); Hummingbird (tiny with fragrant flowers); Pink Spires (with pink flowers); Rosea (has salmon-coloured flowers that become pinkish-white); and Sixteen Candles (which has long white flowers). The only issue with this shrub is spider mites, which you can eliminate with water (or horticultural oils in more severe cases).

Common Name	Wild Azalea, Pinxterbloom
Botanical Name	Rhododendron periclymenoides
Family	Ericaceae
Plant Type	Deciduous shrub
Mature Size	36-240 inches (height and spread)
Sun Exposure	Partial shade
Soil Type	Moist, well-drained
Soil pH	Acidic
Hardiness Zones	3-9 (USDA)
Native Areas	Asia, Europe, North America

Pinxterbloom Azalea is a beautiful addition to your garden if you want to make a floral display. It is dense with pink or white blooms in spring, attracting hummingbirds and butterflies. In autumn, the foliage becomes a dull yellow and is well suited for shrub borders and rain gardens. Its density makes it another contender for privacy screens or hedges in your yard. The form of the Wild Azalea makes it an excellent addition to an informal garden. However, beware of planting this shrub if one of your garden's users will be a cat or dog; if ingested, the plant is poisonous. It can tolerate dry, rocky, sandy soils and the sun in cooler climates. It is a low-maintenance plant, but ensure that you shelter it from strong winter winds and protect it from frost to prevent any damage to the blooms. This shrub is naturally found in swamp margins and moist woods, perfect for regions with plenty of rainfall.

Common Name	Mountain Laurel
Botanical Name	Kalima latifolia
Family	Ericaceae
Plant Type	Shrub
Mature Size	60-180 inches (height and spread)
Sun Exposure	Partial sun
Soil Type	Moist, well-drained
Soil pH	Acidic
Hardiness Zones	4-9 (USDA)
Native Areas	North America

Mountain Laurel is a shrub with beautiful spring blooms of white, pink or rose, and it is attractive throughout the year due to its gnarled stems. It thrives in the shade and usually grows densely and slowly. Mountain Laurel will look lovely planted in shrub borders next to azaleas, rhododendrons, and woodland gardens. It is a brilliant addition to your garden if you wish to attract pollinators such as hummingbirds. However, be careful and considerate of the users of your garden if choosing to plant this, as it is toxic to pets and people if ingested. If selected, you should plant this in a sheltered location from the wind and water it well when the plant is young. Ensure the soil remains moist but it is quite drought-resistant once established. If you experience drought, water your shrub every two to three weeks in spring and once a week in the summer. There are some popular varieties of this shrub, including *K. latifola* Elf (with white flowers); *K. latifola* Minuet (red and white blooms); *K. latifola* Olympic Fire (dark pink blossoms); *K. latifola* Peppermint (white with red stripes); *K. latifola* Firecracker (light pink with red buds); and *K. latifola* Sarah (coral pink). The diseases this plant is prone to are leaf spots, blights, borers, scale, whiteflies, and lace bugs. It can also develop root rot in heavy soils, where you must remove the affected plants.

***

Grass lawn alternatives

Now that we know a list of plants that could work for your climate and their specific needs, let's delve into some alternative options for a big part of many people's yards: the grass lawn. It's essential that you know this because grass does not do well in arid climates with little rainfall;

it can look neglected and reduce the overall appeal of your home.

The first of five options is using decomposed granite as the primary flooring of your landscape. This option is fantastic for areas that do not need to be paved, such as patios, pet areas, and driveways; since it is compacted, there is no dust residue when walking on. Decomposed granite is also a sustainable option. It reduces runoff from rain and irrigation (being absorbent) and filters pollutants from water. Interestingly, this material is high in trace minerals, too, containing essential nutrients for successful and healthy plant growth.

The second option is to plant a meadow of native grasses. One of the many positives of this is the fact that this will add movement to your landscape (if you remember correctly, we said that movement is one of three golden rules for landscaping). The keyword here is 'native', as these species will automatically suit your climate. Plant the same varieties together for a distinct look, grouping them with taller grasses at the back and shorter ones at the front.

Thirdly, you could try pea gravel, which comes in various colours. The most popular choice is neutral, muted tones. There are a few factors to consider when buying pea gravel, including the shape (some types have sharp edges), the size of each rock (some sizes are easier to work with than others), and depth (usually two inches is recommended).

Fourthly, permeable paving. This is considered a sustainable choice as it allows rainwater to sink into the paving, reducing the likelihood of flooding or having waterlogged plants. There are many other benefits to this hardscape, including erosion prevention; moving water away from the house; and reducing the overall contamination of water in rivers, streams, and other water bodies. Common permeable paving types are concrete, asphalt, and interlocking pavers.

The following alternative to a grass lawn is using drought-tolerant groundcovers. We have listed a few of these above, but here are some more you can consider: *Dymondia margaretae; Juniperus; mazus radicans; Monardella macrantha*; and moneywort *Lysimachia nummularia*.

***

How to grow a lawn in dry conditions

If you still desperately want a grass lawn in your backyard, I will teach you how to do it properly. My first tip is to water your lawn under the right conditions. Such conditions include getting the time of day right and ensuring that the weather is agreeable (no to little wind, no rain). You should only water your lawn occasionally, as this encourages the lawn to expect daily watering (and most of the water is evaporated anyway). To effectively water your lawn, you should water it once a week when the sun is rising or setting; by limiting watering, you encourage the plant to send deeper root systems that can utilise the moisture in the soil more effectively.

The second tip is to reduce the footfall on your lawn during summer and minimise your maintenance; taller grass shades the soil and keeps roots cool. During drought, these two things become more extreme; eliminate footfall entirely and do not mow your lawn unless you absolutely must. However, keep the grassroots alive by watering it once if the drought lasts over a month.

Thirdly, there is a right and wrong way to mow your lawn. The right way involves not cutting your grass too short (especially in arid climates) since the blades of grass contain most of the moisture.

Fourthly, suppose you are seeding a new lawn. In that case, you should apply lots of organic material to the soil underneath to help the soil retain moisture. This amended soil will support your new lawn much more effectively than sandy soils, for example, as they drain rapidly. If you have an established lawn, however, you may keep the mulch on the surface of the lawn after you mow it, as this will help retain moisture.

Fire-safe plants to use in your garden

If living in a drought-prone climate, it may be a good idea to consider planting less susceptible to spontaneous combustion (as this causes many wildfires). Please note that no plants are completely fire-resistant. Each plant has its burning rate. The ones we are about to reveal burn slowly, thus buying you more time to deal with the fire before it reaches your property.

Fire-safe plants generally have low maintenance needs and resin content, are low-growing, and do not accumulate many dead leaves and branches. However, if you have not maintained your fire-safe plants correctly, they will no longer be considered fire-safe. The reason for this is that dead matter can easily catch fire.

Some plants, such as succulents, have been recommended due to their high water content. For example, aloes are one of the most fire-resistant plants, particularly the variety of *Aloe arborescens*. Agaves are another succulent that contains water and is a popular plant choice in Southern California (a region notorious for wildfires).

Senecio vitalis (bush blue pickle) is another recommended fire-safe succulent, which you can also use as a water-wise groundcover. The fourth recommendation is *Portulacaria afra* (more commonly known as elephant bush or dwarf jade plant). Interestingly, you can make this plant into a fashionable bonsai, and it will look lovely next to the previous three succulents mentioned above for a 'fire wall of plants'.

The next plant may seem quite unconventional, yet it is known for being fire-resistant. *Fragaria vesca* (wild strawberry or woodland strawberry) is a low-growing plant that also produces small, edible fruit that you can use to make delicious jams and herbal remedies. You can use it as a groundcover, and it does not require much water or maintenance.

French lavender is the next recommendation for many reasons. Besides its sweet fragrance and fire resistance, it also helps prevent erosion. You also do not need to plant so many of these, as it has a three and five inches height and spread, respectively.

The next plant is *Baccharis pilularis* (Coyote bush). This bush has fire-retardant leaves, making them less likely to catch fire. It is also drought-tolerant and native to California, so an excellent choice for anyone who lives there. You can grow it as a groundcover or shrub, depending on your needs and aesthetic preferences.

Our penultimate recommendation is Monkeyflower, which is not only a great firefighter, but also an attractor for Hummingbirds. So with this choice, you protect the environment from harm and provide for the wildlife within it. How poetic.

Lastly, Epilobium canum (California fuchsia), a visually striking plant with bright orange blooms, attracts pollinators in late summer.

It is worth mentioning ice plants, which retain water and have tiny hairs on the surface of their leaves, making them appear as if they sparkle. Despite their water content, they are not recommended for fire-safe planting as the leaves naturally dry, exposing a flammable layer underneath.

***

Drainage

A massive part of designing a climate-conscious garden is ensuring effective drainage. It is critical to keep both your house and yard in excellent form. We will now explore the different ways in which you can achieve adequate drainage for your new garden.

Firstly, you can create a slope by landscape grading so that runoff naturally slides away from your property. Secondly, consider replacing hardscape material with permeable drainage material such as different types of gravel. This will reduce runoff altogether. Thirdly, you could use a rainwater catchment system, like installing a rain barrel next to a downspout. You may repurpose this water later on - a sustainable approach.

Similarly, you could install a catch basin at the end of your downspouts or add downspout extensions to move water around four feet away from your home. Another approach is establishing a channel drain (in your driveway or walkway). Although it may not be the prettiest option, a channel drain will effectively divert water.

Alternatively, you could install a French drain to manage your surface water. It is simply a trench full of porous materials covering a PVC pipe. Again, not very glamorous, but it is inexpensive and effective at keeping water away.

Next, you could aerate your lawn to encourage rain to sink to the roots and reduce runoff. Do this by puncturing holes in the surface, breaking up the underlying compacted soil. This method also benefits your lawn's health, allowing air circulation and nutrients.

The next approach is to build a dry creek bed using a range of rock sizes, from rocks in rivers to small boulders. It will channel the water in a specific direction according to how you arrange the rocks, making it functional and aesthetic.

My penultimate tip is to have a yard drain built into the ground where your yard has previously suffered from flooding. They act the same way as shower drains, channelling water through hidden pipes away from your home.

Lastly, you could build a dry well, an underground basin filled with large rocks. It can hold plenty of water which then percolates to the surrounding soil (which is great if you live in a drought-prone climate, as retaining soil moisture can be an issue).

***

Weather damage

Now we know what to do for drainage, let's tackle the next issue preventing you from having the best garden possible: weather damage. This could range from excessive wind, hail, heatwaves, and drought to snow, frost, storms, and waterlogging. You may know that new plants are more affected by weather events than established plants, but symptoms only show weeks or months after the damage has been done. These symptoms include brown leaves; wilting; scorched leaves; breakage, leaning, or tearing due to wind; creased leaves; bud and leaf drop; and browning of shoots.

To prevent weather damage, consider your climate thoroughly before making a plant selection; choose hardy plants in a region susceptible to extreme cold and frost, and choose drought-tolerant plants if you live in an arid climate. You should also do your best to use any drainage methods we listed before this section to prevent waterlogging. Ensuring good maintenance of your plants will also minimise weather damage, as healthier plants are more resilient.

Let's go more in-depth about ways to weatherproof your garden. Firstly, stabilise your soil and protect it from erosion by adding mulch to your plant beds. Most of the time, it is best to choose organic mulch such as wood chips or bark; inorganic mulches (like plastic) may be excellent at insulating garden beds and battling weeds, but the plastic prevents the crops from receiving water and air. This causes the plant to eventually die after the soil becomes too hot and the roots grow too close to the surface. However, artificial mulch does not get displaced easily by the wind, which is good for preventing erosion.

Speaking of wind, it is helpful to have a windbreak in your garden to protect the plants and elements within. It is as simple as planting a row of trees perpendicular to the direction of the prevailing wind in your region. Just do your tree research, so you know that they will thrive in your garden and can deal with heavy winds. However, trees are only helpful if they are healthy; branches that will fall and break can damage your plant beds below. Another way to protect your plants from strong winds is by covering them with plastic sheets secured with stakes (like pitching a mini, transparent tent). It may not be the most aesthetic option, but at least your budding plants will be safe.

Thirdly, if your area is forecasted for frost, water your plants one day before the freeze (the air temperature should be at least 40 degrees Fahrenheit). Doing this will trap heat in the soil, keeping the roots warm and strengthening your plants in the cold. You can also protect seedlings from frost by covering them with an upturned terracotta pot, insulating them and shielding them from the harsh cold. You can remove the pot once temperatures rise again.

We have mentioned it enough, but I will reinforce the importance of good drainage again. If your soil drains poorly, it will become waterlogged, preventing your plants' roots from receiving necessary oxygen. (Yes, plants need to respire too.) Poor drainage thus will kill your plants (just like if a human was deprived of oxygen for too long). One of the best ways to ensure good soil drainage is to add compost to your soil regularly. Adding compost will attract earthworms, which will helpfully create air pockets in the earth for you, massively boosting drainage.

To protect your garden from hailstorms, lay a tarp over your garden beds, securing them with sticks or hoops staked into the soil. To protect vertical plantings, lean a plywood sheet against the vertical surface where your plants are growing to act as a shield, ensuring you secure it with a weight to prevent the sheet from blowing away (if you are also experiencing heavy winds).

You are now well-equipped with knowledge about the effects of weather on your garden and how to protect it!

5
Sustainable Solutions in Garden Design

This chapter covers a topic I am most passionate about - sustainability. I will highlight the importance of designing your garden in this way so that I can inspire you to do your part for the precious planet we live in. We touched on sustainable solutions in chapter three, but this is where you will fully understand and appreciate the necessity of designing your garden sustainably. At the end of the chapter, you will realise there is no other logical way to design your garden other than in this fashion.

In short, a sustainable garden should: conserve water; use a native plant selection; mimic natural ecosystems; provide food (and possibly habitats) for wildlife; and use organic fertiliser. Let us delve into these points.

In chapter four, we discussed suitable plant selections for your regional climate. Notice that most plant species mentioned were native; as you must know by now, choosing native plants is the more sustainable option because they will grow much more easily, require less maintenance, and will not require international transportation to get to your garden. Additionally, plants growing in their native climate are unlikely to need supplementary watering from irrigation as they will be adapted to the natural water systems in their region. They will also be more pest and disease-resistant, making it easier to maintain a problem-free garden. The carbon emissions saved from these three factors alone are immensely significant.

A reliable way of preventing disease and pests from taking over your plants is to plant many different plants in one location. For example, having a mixture of flowers, herbs, and vegetable plant beds neighbouring each other disallows pests from finding their targeted plant. This is because their eyeline will be disrupted with many other plant species that the pest will not be targeting. Certain herbs can also help to control pests, such as Foeniculum (Fennel) and Anethum (Dill), which attract beneficial insects. Similarly, flowers such as Achillea (Yarrow) and Rudbeckia (coneflower) attract helpful insects. Likewise, you should also rotate the location of your plant selection year after year; this will prevent any buildup of fungal diseases and pests from ruining your plants.

Another vital element of creating a sustainable garden is balancing inputs (water, fossil fuels, fertiliser) and outputs (flowers, fruit, vegetables, waste, runoff). One easy way to do this is composting. Compost turns garden waste (such as fruit and vegetable peel) into nutrients for the soil, encouraging healthy plant growth and making your garden functional and visually appealing. Another example of balancing inputs and outputs is collecting rainwater for irrigation. Another way to make your garden more sustainable is to limit or eliminate the use of unnatural pesticides; instead, use organic fertilisers from plants or animals.

Sustainable garden design has numerous benefits, including elevating your garden's aesthetic appeal and functionality. In a sustainable garden, all the elements work together holistically to produce a beautiful working system that pleases the user and gives back to the environment. To make your garden sustainable, start by considering how you can imitate natural systems with the elements you want your garden to have. This can be as simple as mimicking a wildflower meadow by including native pollinator plants in a small section of your garden; it is beautiful and natural, giving back to the environment by providing nectar for the ecosystem. In addition, by providing for birds, you attract them to your garden, which helps the ecosystem and you in multiple ways. For example, birds can help prevent unwanted insect visitors from eating plants since many birds feed on insects.

***

Biomimicry

You can also imitate nature through permaculture, which means using various plant materials to mimic what is naturally found in healthy, natural ecosystems such as forests and meadows. Permaculture in a garden can include a mixture of herbs, pollinator plants, shrubs, trees, fungi, and plants to attract animals such as rabbits and deer. The diverse ecosystem you create ensures that each user of your yard makes a valuable contribution to the health of your garden, just like animals and insects naturally help forests to thrive. A layered and diverse planting scheme suited to your climate and garden will create a long-lasting, abundant ecosystem. Your garden will then become a self-regulating system that requires minimal maintenance to stay healthy.

Part of the biomimicry process is to allow plants to compete. In other words, let the strongest and most suitable plants thrive, and the weaker, less appropriate plants fall. The competition between plants occurs in natural places like woodlands and meadows, so the key to this concept is not to be overly protective of your plants. Instead, let nature take its course by allowing plants to self-seed and others to be shaded.

Another way to mimic nature in your garden is to allow for natural composting; when leaves fall in autumn, let them decompose into rich organic matter. You can also collect these dead plant materials and place them in strategic areas (such as atop certain plant beds) to use as mulch, reducing the need to water.

We can also employ techniques to mimic a forest floor in our garden. One approach is called 'lasagne gardening' (sheet composting). This method layers compostable, organic materials on top of each other within a flat-surfaced plant bed. Layers may include newspaper, cardboard, grass clippings, tea leaves/bags, coffee grounds, fruit and vegetable peel, and garden trimmings. The only organic material you should avoid is pest and disease-ridden plant material, which may cause issues in your new garden. The two-foot tall bed will decompose into nutrient-rich compost within two to four weeks.

The second technique is the 'Hugelkultur mound', meaning hill mound. Plants are grown on a raised bed with a mounded form. Similar to the lasagna bed process, hugelkulturs are made from plant debris and partially rotten woody material layered underneath compost and soil. It results in a mound of about five to six feet, but after lots of decomposition, the pile shrinks to about two feet tall. A hugelkulter mound is terrific at providing long-term nutrients to your plants. The wood stores rainwater that is released in drier periods. It is a sponge ecosystem where helpful organisms live (like a natural forest floor). The hugelkultur also extends the growing season by generating heat, so they are ideal spaces to plant some vegetables (particularly cucumbers, potatoes, melons, legumes, and squashes).

Another note on mimicking nature is to choose organic shapes, forms, and lines. We covered this more in-depth in chapter one; nature hardly uses straight lines, so if you want to mimic nature in your garden, use curves, circles, and spirals when designing your landscape. It would also help to keep your material palette natural only, such as stone, gravel, and wood.

Lastly, make the most of trees; they provide habitat, food, shelter, and shade, enrich the soil, store water, and can act as a windbreak. The many services a tree can provide in your garden mean that they are an ecosystem. Therefore, they should be valued and used wisely in your garden to attract wildlife and encourage a more diverse ecosystem within your yard.

***

Creating a wildlife meadow

Meadows are a sustainable addition to your garden because they are filled with plant diversity and support a range of animal life. This includes microorganisms, bees, birds, and butterflies. Depending on your garden size and plant selection, your meadow may help restore your local biodiversity's habitat. In this way, designing a wildlife meadow in your garden can improve your local ecology; natives attract native insects, which attract native birds. This creates a valuable habitat. To help you plan your sustainable wildflower meadow, I have compiled a list of native plants (to the U.S. and Canada).

Common Name	Black-Eyed Susan
Botanical Name	Rubeckia hirta
Family	Asteraceae
Plant Type	Perennial
Mature Size	24-36 inches (height) 12-24 inches (spread)
Sun Exposure	Full sun
Soil Type	Dry to moist, well-drained
Soil pH	Acidic, neutral
Hardiness Zones	3-9 (USDA)
Native Areas	North America (eastern two-thirds)

Black-Eyed Susan attracts bordered patch butterflies (Chlosyne lacinia) and Gorgone checkerspot butterflies (Chlosyne Gorgone) with a bright appearance of yellow flowers and brown centres. It usually grows in prairies and becomes drought-tolerant once established. It can stand out when used in mass plantings such as a meadow.

Common Name	Blue Vervain
Botanical Name	Verbena hastata
Family	Verbenaceae
Plant Type	Perennial, Annual
Mature Size	24-72 inches (height) 12-30 inches (spread)
Sun Exposure	Full sun, partial shade, full shade
Soil Type	Moist or wet, well-drained
Soil pH	Acidic, neutral
Hardiness Zones	3-8 (USDA)
Native Areas	North America, Canada

Blue Vervain has pleasantly purple-coloured flowers that can self-seed and quickly spread. Due to its soil conditions, this plant is beneficial in a rain garden and can attract bees, birds, and butterflies.

Common Name	Butterflyweed
Botanical Name	Asclepias tuberosa
Family	Asclepiadaceae
Plant Type	Herbaceous perennial
Mature Size	12-24 inches (height) 12-18 inches (spread)
Sun Exposure	Full sun
Soil Type	Dry, well-drained
Soil pH	Slightly acidic to neutral
Hardiness Zones	3-9 (USDA)
Native Areas	North America (eastern and southeastern), Canada

Butterflyweed has clusters of deep orange flowers that bloom from May to September. These attract monarch butterflies and caterpillars, leafcutter bees, cuckoo bees, sweat bees, and small carpenter bees. They are commonly found growing in prairies, meadows, and forest clearings. Once established, this species is drought-tolerant and can adapt to many soil types with good drainage.

Common Name	Common Self-Heal
Botanical Name	Prunella vulgaris
Family	Lamiaaceae
Plant Type	Herbaceous perennial
Mature Size	12 inches (height) 8 inches (spread)
Sun Exposure	Full sun, partial shade
Soil Type	Moist, well-drained
Soil pH	Slightly acidic to neutral
Hardiness Zones	4-8 (USDA)
Native Areas	North America, Europe, Asia

Common Self-Heal is a herb belonging to the mint family and sprouts blue-purple flowers that attract the clouded sulphur butterfly (Colias philodice). Sometimes, the flowers appear pink or white. This plant can adapt to different soil conditions but grows better in moist soils. As well as in the wildflower meadow, Common Self-Heal can be grown as a groundcover.

Common Name	Common Yarrow
Botanical Name	Achillea millefolium
Family	Asteraaceae
Plant Type	Perennial
Mature Size	18-24 inches (height) 12-24 inches (spread)
Sun Exposure	Full sun
Soil Type	Dry to moist, well-drained
Soil pH	Neutral
Hardiness Zones	3-9 (USDA)
Native Areas	North America, Asia, Europe

Common Yarrow usually blooms with pink or white flowers that attract many pollinators, including hoverflies, bees, birds, butterflies, moths, beneficial insects, and more. However, this plant is toxic to cats, dogs, and horses if ingested, so be wary of the users of your garden before deciding to include this in your meadow. It is also considered an "aggressive weed". However, when used in a mass planting, the form becomes more exciting and can stand out. This perennial is drought-tolerant once established and can thrive even in poor soil, making it a perfect addition to your xeriscape (if you live in an arid climate).

Common Name	Fall Sneezeweed
Botanical Name	Helenium autumnale
Family	Asteraceae
Plant Type	Perennial
Mature Size	24-60 inches (height) 24 inches (spread)
Sun Exposure	Full sun
Soil Type	Moist, well-drained
Soil pH	Acidic to neutral
Hardiness Zones	3-8 (USDA)
Native Areas	North America, southern Canada

This stunning perennial blooms fiery orange flowers with a splash of yellow at the edges of the petals. They usually grow in low-lying meadows or damp woodland edges and attract butterflies in late summer through autumn, making them the perfect plant to grow in a wildflower meadow. They love moisture and will not grow well in a drought-prone climate. Just ensure that you give them enough air circulation to prevent any fungal rot from developing. Some of the most interesting varieties of Helenium include Adios (yellow petals with purple edges); Beatrice, Butterpat, El Dorado (yellow petals); Red-Haired Katy (crimson petals); and Waldtraut (sunset orange petals).

Common Name	Fireweed
Botanical Name	Chamerion angustifolium
Family	Onagraceae
Plant Type	Perennial
Mature Size	24-108 inches (height) 12-36 inches (spread)
Sun Exposure	Full sun, partial shade
Soil Type	Moist, rich, well-drained
Soil pH	Acidic
Hardiness Zones	2-7 (USDA)
Native Areas	North America, Canada, Europe, Asia

This perennial gets its name from its ability to rapidly regrow after a wildfire has burned the landscape. It will produce tiny, pretty magenta flowers from summer to autumn. It grows best in organically rich soil but can adapt to different moisture levels. Fireweed is a clever addition to your landscape if you wish to wow your viewers; when grown in large masses, the magenta petals are outstanding. Naturally, Fireweed grows alongside grasses and sedges, so you may want to mimic this combination in your meadow. Of course, this is a marvellous plant for pollinators, being a larval host for a particular moth species, the Hyles lineata (also known as the white-lined sphinx moth). It also attracts hummingbirds and long-tongued bees.

Common Name	Gray Goldenrod
Botanical Name	Solidago nemoralis
Family	Asteraceae
Plant Type	Herbaceous perennial
Mature Size	18-60 inches (height) 12-36 inches (spread)
Sun Exposure	Full sun, partial shade
Soil Type	Dry to medium-dry, average, poor, infertile, well-drained
Soil pH	Acidic, neutral
Hardiness Zones	2-8 (USDA)
Native Areas	North America

As a sunflower family member, this perennial has yellow flowers and looks lovely in cottage gardens. It is a very low-maintenance plant that will grow well in any sunny spot. It is also unaffected by pests and diseases unless the air circulation around the plant is insufficient. In this case, it can get rust fungus, leaf spots, and powdery mildew. This species is an aggressive spreader; however, some varieties are not aggressive, including *Soldiago caesia* (blue-stemmed goldenrod) and *Soldiago odora* (sweet goldenrod). Gray Goldenrod will also provide for bees (long and short-tongued); wasps; flies; beetles; butterflies; moths; and caterpillars.

Common Name	Jerusalem Artichoke, sunchoke, sunroot
Botanical Name	Helianthus tuberosus
Family	Asteraceae
Plant Type	Herbaceous perennial
Mature Size	72-120 inches (height) 36-60 inches (spread)
Sun Exposure	Full sun, partial shade
Soil Type	Moist, well-drained
Soil pH	Acidic
Hardiness Zones	3-9 (USDA)
Native Areas	North America

This is another wildflower related to sunflowers with yellow petals and green-yellow centres blooming in summer. This plant can be drought-tolerant once established and adapt to different soil moisture levels as long as it is drained well. One inch of water weekly is sufficient to enable healthy growth. As well as providing for pollinators, Jersalen artichokes also cater for humans by producing potato-like root vegetables. Furthermore, they can provide shelter from the wind for more of your sensitive plants due to their height and strength. The only problems encountered with this plant are the slugs and aphids that feed on them, but you can prevent this if you manage your weeds well. This wildflower attracts a range of bee species (such as bumblebees, cuckoo bees, digger bees, leaf-cutting bees, halictid bees, and andenid bees), making it a wildlife hotspot. In addition, Sunchoke attracts many butterfly species, such as the

Gorgone Checkerspot; Silvery Checkerspot; Painted Lady, and various moth species (Arge Tiger moth and Ruby Tiger moth).

Common Name	Nodding Onion
Botanical Name	Allium cernuum
Family	Amaryllidaceae
Plant Type	Herbaceous perennial
Mature Size	12-24 inches (height) 3-6 inches (spread)
Sun Exposure	Full sun, partial shade
Soil Type	Dry to slightly moist, well-drained
Soil pH	Alkaline
Hardiness Zones	4-8 (USDA)
Native Areas	North America

The Nodding Onion plant is a small species that produce dangling purple, pink, or occasionally white flowers in the summertime. Due to its size, it is best shown at the front of a plant mass and should be planted in groups to give some visual impact. They look delightful in rock and cottage gardens and attract bees, butterflies, moths, beneficial insects, and other pollinators. However, consider the users of your garden before deciding on this plant, as it is toxic to cats, dogs, and horses if ingested. Nodding onion grows well in full sun and hotter climates, often found in woods, prairies, and coastal bluffs.

Common Name	Purple Coneflower
Botanical Name	Echinacea purpurea
Family	Asteraceae
Plant Type	Herbaceous perennial
Mature Size	24-60 inches (height) 12-24 inches (spread)
Sun Exposure	Full sun, partial shade
Soil Type	Well-drained
Soil pH	Acidic to neutral
Hardiness Zones	3-8 (USDA)
Native Areas	North America

Purple Coneflower blooms petals of a purple-pink colour in summer, attracting many pollinators with its orange centres. These include several bee species (honey bees, leafcutter bees) and butterfly species (Monarchs, Tiger Swallowtails, Skippers, Red Admirals, American Ladies, and Fritillaries); it is also a larval host for the Silvery Checkerspot butterfly caterpillars. Goldfinches and songbirds also benefit from this plant. Once established, Purple Coneflower becomes drought-tolerant and may only need watering during droughts. It also is reasonably disease-free, as long as you ensure good air circulation (like with every other plant we mentioned) to prevent fungal rot. Therefore, this is another low-maintenance plant to add to your selection.

Common Name	Wild Bergamot, Bee Balm
Botanical Name	Monarda fistulosa
Family	Lamiaceae
Plant Type	Herbaceous perennial
Mature Size	10-48 inches (height) 10-36 inches (spread)
Sun Exposure	Full sun, partial
Soil Type	Rich, moist
Soil pH	Acidic to neutral
Hardiness Zones	3-9 (USDA)
Native Areas	North America

The Bee Balm plant is a superb addition to a cottage garden and wildflower meadow. Able to handle various soil conditions, the flower produces purple and pink blooms from summer to autumn and attracts bees and butterflies, acting as a larval host to the Raspberry Pyrausta butterfly. Hummingbirds also gain value from this plant, and its fragrance is very pleasurable for humans. However, be careful of its self-seeding nature, as it is known as an aggressive spreader. Also, this plant may be subject to powdery mildew, so ensure proper maintenance measures.

With this selection of gorgeous native plants, you can create your own sustainable wildflower meadow in your backyard. Many of these plants grow well together, so I put them in the same selection. All you have to do is plant them at the right time of year under the right conditions and look after them.

As well as including a wildlife meadow for pollinators, why not create a wildlife pond for aquatic biodiversity? A pond is a water feature and can be a relaxing focal point in your garden. It is another excellent way to add movement and life to your yard. If you are going for an informal, natural-looking garden that really mimics nature, why not consider a log pile too? Log piles will provide food for local wildlife, such as birds, toads, newts, bees, and insects.

***

Water-saving techniques

With the imminent threat of climate change and the increased severity of weather events (like droughts and wildfires), we should be doing everything in our power to conserve our most precious natural resource: water.

In previous chapters, we covered a few water-saving tips (like installing rainwater catchment systems, drip irrigation systems, reusing greywater, using mulch, and planting native and drought-resistant plants). However, there are a couple more ways to save this precious commodity through careful planning.

Firstly, make use of self-watering baskets. These hanging baskets keep a reservoir of water for when the soil in the basket dries out. The water is then absorbed by the roots when needed; you must check the water level occasionally, ensuring it is topped up when it looks low. This method is a fine low-maintenance solution for those gardeners who are low on time or are forgetful. You will not have to worry about over or underwatering your plants ever again!

Secondly, minimise water loss by preparing your planters. If you plan to pot some of your outdoor plants, they will need their own care. Ceramic planters are often porous and absorb the water for your potted plant. To prevent this unnecessary water loss, treat the inside of your planters with a waterproofer. You may also use water-absorbent crystals in pots to increase the soil's ability to retain moisture. The crystals are helpful because they release water slowly when the plant's roots need to drink. However, water crystals are less successful when used in outdoor containers than indoor ones (mainly due to weather conditions such as drought).

Part of being sustainable is reusing and keeping some elements in your garden. In other words, it means not stripping your garden down to build it back up again. This notion is not limited to hardscape; it also considers keeping some existing softscape. Some mature trees and shrubs you may have could be part of a species habitat or shelter, so getting rid of them is unhelpful to your local wildlife. Even if you do not find wildlife in your garden, it could pass through some of your existing vegetation. If this is the case, try to keep this part of your yard and make design changes around it not to disturb the wildlife. (Heath, 2018) A good starting point is to clean up your yard before eliminating elements that may be ecologically beneficial. Getting rid of weeds and doing some maintenance will clear your judgement and make it easier to see what can stay and must go.

***

Easy and quick ways to instantly transform your yard

One trick that will transform the look of your current yard is to reshape your flower beds. For example, if you currently have linear beds and are yearning for a more relaxed, natural feel, why not introduce organic shapes and curves? Curves will instantly change the look and feel of your landscape and do not cost much time or money. Also note that straight beds can make your yard look smaller, while curves add the illusion of a larger space. You can also use old bricks to outline your new plant beds by laying a path embedded in gravel, giving your beds a patterned edge.

Another method of revamping your yard in a sustainable way is by covering up a weathered deck with an outdoor rug. This will instantly brighten up your existing patio and does not cost a fortune. If you choose a patterned rug, it is also a focal point for arranging your garden furniture around. Investing in a rug is a simple way to freshen up your patio. If this does not appeal to you, why not try painting your old patio floor with a stylish pattern? A remarkable floor will contrast nicely against your outdoor furniture and accessories and breathe new life into your social area.

Thirdly, you could paint your fences and garden walls a new colour depending on the mood you are trying to create. For example, if you are after a natural look, you may want to paint the fences a neutral shade, such as a pastel colour. Use bright, bold colours like yellows and oranges to uplift the atmosphere. If you want the illusion of a more extensive garden, use dark green, black and green-grey. These colours will help your plants stand out and become a lovely backdrop to your outdoor furniture.

Furthermore, repainting your garden boundaries gives your garden a fresh look and can be completed in a day. You can also repaint your shed to brighten up your yard easily. However, if painting (or repainting) elements is not attractive to you, you can add colour by framing succulents. This is the idea of growing succulents within a picture frame which you can hang vertically. This living artwork will take your garden to a new level, especially if you decorate a whole wall with them. It may even become a feature wall for your garden.

Fourthly, if you currently have a pathway through your garden (and you like its current location but not the look of it), why not use either gravel, shingle, or wood chippings to give it a new lease of life? How about some beautiful log slices for stepping stones? These are quick and straightforward to do independently and instantly add character to your garden.

A fifth idea to quickly revamp your garden space is to add a focal point. If you like the look of your current yard but feel that something is missing, it may need a focal point to pull viewers in. It could be as simple as adding a water feature or an interesting, eye-catching plant form as part of your plant mass. You could even use your newly painted wall (as discussed above) as a destination point. You may even consider painting a mural on your wall to add artwork to your garden. However, the last thing you want to do is confuse viewers with too many focal points; it is best to stick with one or two within the whole garden.

Another sustainable solution to your dreary-looking garden problem is to upcycle any wooden pallets you own and use them as garden furniture; this works particularly well in an informal or cottage garden. Your old wooden pallet can be repurposed as a useful garden table with a fresh lick of paint to give it a new look. If you paint it a bright colour, your seating area will suddenly look more cheerful. A second item you can upcycle is old wooden crates; upturn and stack them to create stylish garden shelves, perfect for a plant display or storing Wellington boots and other garden accessories. It is worth noting that they may fall over if not secured to a fence or each other. Not only will this repurpose old crates lying around, but it will also immediately add organisation to your landscape. You can also create garden shelves by repurposing old ladders; two can form an 'A' shape, tied together at the top with a wooden plank laid horizontally atop the runs on either side to make shelves. This will look charming, decorated with small plant pots and garden accessories against a stone wall.

You may also repurpose old pots and pans to use as planters. All you need to do is create a few holes at the bottom for drainage, and you can use them to grow your plants in. Planters like this will give your garden a rustic feel and fit perfectly into an informal garden. Furthermore, the durable shells of cooking pots make them suitable for the outdoors.

Repurposing items is one thing, and multi-purposing is another. To save space, money, and resources, you could use your garden shed as a bar during warmer months to entertain guests. Multi-purposing is a perfect solution for those who do not want to remake their whole garden to accommodate guests and social events. Your shed can function as a storage area in the winter and open into a bar setting for garden parties in summer. You can be as creative as you like with this, hanging herb planters from the roof for decoration or use in drinks. Hanging floral baskets is another way to increase your yard's appeal with minimal effort. If you like the idea of repurposing your shed, you can alternatively convert it into an art studio, a cute summerhouse, or even an indoor play area for children.

Speaking of garden furniture, the following could be an excellent idea for those of you who are DIY-savvy (or have a friend that could help you out if you are not). Consider making your garden furniture if you want to add a seating area to your current garden. You could buy some MDF boards from your local retailer and create a corner sofa connected to a couple of garden walls. Paint it in trendy colours that go with the rest of your garden style, and ensure to varnish your seat to make it waterproof. Adorn the seat with many outdoor cushions for a final touch of cosiness. If you have a neutral tones garden colour palette, don't be afraid to add a pop of colour using your cushions. You could even add a coffee table and outdoor lighting to make the social area come alive.

To accessorise your garden sustainably, you could bring some indoor accessories to the outdoors. Rather than spending a fortune adorning your outdoor furniture with specially bought items, you literally could make your garden an extension of your home by dressing it up with indoor textile decoration. Not only is this a trend, but it's also non-permanent; when the weather turns for the worst, you can easily bring your accessories back indoors to safety. Furthermore, this means you can try new looks with different indoor accessories each time, giving your garden different characteristics.

The next point is for those who want to grow their own food but need more space with your garden's current layout. Well, worry no more, my friends. Who says vegetables must be grown in the ground? You could create a vegetable trug instead! Trugs are awesome accessories to have in your garden; they are both ornamental and practical as they have a variety of uses (one of them being allowing you to harvest your own fruit and veg). They are also ideal for herb planting; growing companion plants alongside your veggies will keep pests at bay. The only downside to using a trug to grow food is that you need to water it regularly and cannot rely on your regional rain patterns to be sufficient. However, growing your own food in a trug is still more sustainable than redoing your entire garden from scratch and buying your food from the supermarket.

The last idea benefits your local wildlife and upgrades your garden atmosphere. Attracting birds to your yard using a bird feeder will bring a sense of serenity and relaxation; hearing the birds chirping will enhance the ambience of your garden and, in turn, make you feel happier too. Over time, listening to birds chirping can boost your mood and improve your overall mental health. With all these positive outcomes, it seems illogical not to add one to your existing garden.

So now you know the innumerable ways to make your garden sustainable, whether you are beginning a new design or adding interest to your existing garden. From choosing the correct planting and planning irrigation zones to upcycling furniture and making DIY garden elements, you are well-equipped with the knowledge of being more sustainable. So let's save the planet one garden at a time!

6
Delightful Design Ideas For All Budgets

With the topic of sustainability safely under our belts, we can move on to designing your dream garden on a budget that works for you. Many examples mentioned above work exceptionally well for those on a low budget. As you already know, before you begin designing or redesigning your yard, you should have already set a budget of how much you are willing to spend on this project. This applies to everyone, whether you can afford to splash the cash or not.

Most people spend most of their garden makeover budget on hardscape elements (around 70-80%). You should therefore have the right mindset when designing your dream garden; think of it as an investment that will provide you with countless benefits for many years to come. A well-designed garden will be valued between 8 and 15% of the value of your home. It will definitely increase the value of your home if done correctly. You can use this to estimate how much you should spend on your garden.

Let's begin by exploring different choices of hardscape elements you may wish to consider. Each one works for a different budget type, so you will have to choose the best features for you. We can split it into four categories, the first of which is functional garden structures.

Functional garden structures

1. An **arbour** is a popular hardscape element in a garden. It is a small, semi-enclosed structure used as a resting place and will typically include seating shaded by vegetation, such as shrubs, vines, or trees. They were historically used in Egyptian gardens and throughout Europe.

2. A **pavilion** is another shelter designed initially for relaxation. However, modern pavilions can have many uses depending on your intention; they can be highly social spaces for hosting parties, group activities, and even community gatherings. Therefore, they can be small or large structures adapted to any budget.

3. A **trellis** is a small hardscape element that displays

and trains climbing plants. Depending on your garden layout and design intention, they can be standalone or attached to a wall. For example, you can use trellis archways as a decorative entrance to the garden.

4. A **pergola** connects elements of the built environment, such as your home, to your garden. It often features columns supporting a trellis roof typically used to shade a walkway. You can use the trellis feature to grow vines or climbing plants, adding interest to the hardscape.

5. A **belvedere** is a place in the garden for people to sit and appreciate a view. They are usually situated on a higher level, but you can still enjoy the view within your garden on the ground level. They are commonly found in English gardens.

6. A **conservatory** is usually found in estate gardens for those on a higher budget. They are made of glass and metal to enjoy your garden surroundings and natural light while being sheltered from the elements.

7. A **folly** is a non-practical hardscape element

usually used for decoration. Follies often mimic old ruins and are used as focal points and garden ornaments. They were historically popular in English and French gardens.

8. A **gazebo** is an ornamental feature that can function as a sheltered place to stand and admire the view of your garden. It can also feature seating and was popular in Roman and Egyptian gardens in the past.

9. A **greenhouse** is a glass structure used to cultivate plants under controlled conditions. They are more a practical than ornamental addition to the garden and are not recommended for those on a low budget.

***

Ornamental structures

The next type of hardscape is ornamental.

1. A **jardinière** is an artistically designed container used for growing plants. It is usually found in

herb gardens and is typically made from ceramic.

2. An **obelisk** is a long, vertical object that you can use as a focal point or to indicate the garden's centre. The base is square-shaped and tapers to a pyramid at the top. They were historically used in Egyptian temples and will fit nicely into a formal garden setting.

3. **Statues** also work well in formal gardens and can be made from various materials, including stone, copper, ceramic, glass, and concrete. You can choose the material that works for your budget if a statue is a hardscape element you desire in your dream garden.

***

Hardscape for animals

The third hardscape type is for animals.

1. An **apiary** (usually wooden) structure keeps beehives for honey creation.

2. An **aviary** is used to house birds with enough space for them to fly. However, keeping birds in an enclosure is not a sustainable way to look after them, in my opinion. Instead, I recommend naturally attracting them to your garden by providing bird feeders and planting vegetation offering beneficial fruit and pollen.

3. A **piscina** is a small pond dedicated to accommodating fish, often used to decorate a garden. A piscina is for those with a medium to high budget, as maintaining the pond and wildlife within will be a costly undertaking.

***

Water structures

Let's now take a look at common water structures.

1. A **chadar** has a rough, sloped surface over which water flows, creating pleasant sounds in the garden. They are commonly found in courtyard gardens today.

2. A **rill** is a small channel carved into stone or concrete to direct water to a specific location, like plant beds, although they can be decorative too. They were previously used in Persian gardens and can be found today in the layout of Islamic gardens. It is, therefore, best used in formal garden styles as they typically use linear lines.

3. A **water wall** is a perforated wall that allows water to seep through for a calming sound and visually pleasing effect. They can also be practical water features, enabling buried pipes to drain their groundwater.

4. A **jub** is a lower-budget and beneficial water feature in your garden, especially in an arid climate. Trees are planted in a hollow to discourage evaporation and allow trees to have the most access to water. This excellent water conservation technique was commonly used in Persian gardens.

5. A **berm** is another affordable option, beneficial for gardeners who need erosion control. It is an earth mound that easily adds variety to a landscape by changing the levels in your garden.

They are functional and aesthetic, able to divert surface runoff and prevent erosion. They can also create hidden views and sound barriers within the garden, instantly adding interest. You may also wish to highlight some plants or rocks by placing them on the berm.

6. A **pond** can suit both high and lower-budget gardens. The simplest ponds will have pebbles surrounding a small cavity in the ground, filled with water atop the pond liner. You can attract wildlife and add an aesthetic here by planting water-loving plants.

***

Softscape

Now that you know the common hardscape structures, let's examine some high- and low-end softscape elements.

1. An **allée** is a linear pathway (typically made of gravel or grass) with shrubs or trees planted symmetrically on either side. The end of the allée usually has a decorative hardscape element, such

as a statue or fountain. An allée is most suitable for more extensive gardens with a formal design intent.

2. A **bower** is a garden shelter made from tree branches or vines that have grown together in a twisted fashion. They are functional and decorative, usually including a place to sit.

3. **Carpet bedding** is a mass of low-growing plants arranged geometrically atop a lawn. It is a technique best suited to bigger yards, where the patterns can be appreciated on a larger scale. Also known as pictorial gardening, this was previously used in Victorian English gardens.

4. **Espalier** is a technique used to grow trees in a pattern on a trellis. It is a great space-saving technique and is suited to smaller gardens. Espalier trees grow fruit much faster than traditionally grown trees because the walls against which they are grown retain the sun's heat. Formal patterns are often used in espalier, known as diamond, candelabra, tiered, fan, and weave.

5. You may use **perennial borders** in any garden

type, which refers to a diverse collection of plants closely planted along a garden edge or pathway. This softscape design adds visual appeal by carefully arranging perennials and shrubs for variety and colour.

6. A **knot garden** is for those of you with huge backyards because it involves a geometric pattern that is best appreciated on a large scale. The pattern consists of low hedges or a selection of fragrant plants and herbs, usually with gravel pathways in between. Depending on your design intent, it can be as elaborate or as simple as you like. However, this softscape suits formal gardens.

7. A **parterre** is similar to a knot garden because it involves a geometric pattern. The difference is that this geometric pattern comprises plant beds surrounded by low hedges or pathways made from stone or gravel. Again, the design is best suited to larger-scale gardens to be appreciated.

8. **Pollard trees** have been pruned, forming a ball-like shape on the remaining branch heads. You can pollard trees in any garden to make your

tree more compact and closer to the ground. It also restricts the canopy's spread, which can be particularly helpful in smaller gardens where you want to reduce shade cover.

9. A **potager** is a separate garden area dedicated to growing fruit and vegetables, which may include herbs and flowers. The idea is to make food cultivation look visually appealing, so plants are often grown for their form and colour to create an ornamental display. This type of softscape works in both formal and informal garden settings; for example, as a knot garden or cottage garden.

10. **Topiary** is when trees and shrubs have been clipped into sculptures or geometric shapes. They have been used in cottage and estate gardens, but consider your design intention before including this as part of your softscape. It may look out of place in a small, informal backyard. It also may need regular maintenance to keep it looking tidy.

With your newfound knowledge of the most common types of garden elements, you can decide which ones suit your budget (and garden size) the most. Remember your design goal when choosing elements from these lists; the last thing you want is mismatched features that do not work together.

***

Small budget ideas

If you have decided that your garden design budget is relatively small, do not fret that your garden won't be as beautiful as you imagined. With a few design tips and tricks, your garden will look completely redone. We have already mentioned some lower-budget tips in the chapter about designing sustainably, so I will cover other ideas below.

> 1. One smart way to save money is to swap stone or brick pathways for self-binding gravel (or any gravel); it is cheaper both in the cost of material and labour. Speaking of labour, ensure to negotiate with any landscape professionals you want to hire. You may get a better deal than what they initially offered. If you really want to save money, though, you can redesign most of the garden yourself. Take time to consider what must be done by a professional, as labour can add up to

over half of the total cost of your project.

2. Another way to save money is to compare the prices of your desired elements from different retailers. It may sound obvious, but many people fail to do their research correctly, resulting in them paying a higher price than necessary. You could also visit recycling centres and reclamation yards for garden containers and tools.

3. Thirdly, wisely choose when to purchase certain plants as the prices vary throughout the year. For example, bulbs and bare-root plants are most affordable in autumn; hedging plants and bare-root trees are cheaper to buy in the dormant season.

4. Consider tiered planters if you have a small garden and want to maximise floor space. These are very inexpensive yet pretty and practical, letting you grow a range of plants in a hierarchical fashion. It also adds levels to your landscape, making it more interesting. You can even repurpose an old ladder rather than buy a tiered planter if you really want to save every penny (and make a sustainable choice).

5. Similarly, you can incorporate vertical gardening to save space. Vertical gardening uses plants that grow upwards rather than outwards, such as climbers. You may also consider making privacy screens from densely growing shrubs trained to a wall or hedges of a certain height. Using trained vegetation is an excellent way to save money on hardscape for privacy.

6. Another space-saving technique is to use fold-up garden furniture. This type of furniture is a great way to reduce clutter when the weather changes and outdoor activities cease. Suitable for smaller gardens, it is also an inexpensive way to make the most of your yard.

7. The next idea helps to create the illusion of a bigger yard. If you have garden slabs, try laying them out diagonally; this will trick the eye and elongate the space. Also, choose a grouting one shade lighter than the paving to ensure it does not visually dominate your yard. Furthermore, if you have existing paving, it may be worth using a pressure washer to brighten your garden.

8. Another design idea suitable for smaller gardens

is strong, bold, linear lines. Although this is the opposite of a natural look and imitating nature, definitive lines can give small gardens a stylish look. This is especially true when this concept is married with changing the materiality, creating different 'zones'. Furthermore, adding curves and organic shapes to a more miniature garden can eat into extra space compared to using straight lines. Also, curves are typically harder to fabricate, making them more expensive to incorporate.

9. The eighth design idea is to use containers to grow plants. Not only will this save floor space, but it also adds so much character to a garden without flowers. So even if the primary use of your garden is to entertain guests, use container gardening to bring life to the social area; it is handy for patios, decks, and paved areas. This technique can also be wildlife-friendly if you choose to include pollinator plants.

10. Another low-budget idea (which also is sustainable) is reusing plastic bottles as planters. They can look decorative, filled with compost and adorned with your pretty plants. In addition, they are better for the environment since plastic does

not biodegrade. It also saves money from buying containers or baskets to hang your plants in.

11. Adding a tree to your garden is always a good idea, no matter the size of your yard. It is an instant, eco-friendly way of making your garden look more enticing and is a worthwhile, inexpensive investment. Just be sure to know your site conditions and regional climate before choosing any tree, as well as the tree's growth requirements; the last thing we want is for the tree to take over your yard because its height and spread were not considered.

12. Another money-saving design idea is to invest in a selection of plant types for yearly interest. Using plants that produce fruit and flowers and change colours with the seasons is recommended for visual appeal and the value added to your local biodiversity. It is also more sustainable to use a varied plant selection of shrubs, grasses, annuals and herbaceous perennials because of the benefits that plant diversity brings to your garden. Furthermore, these plants will last for many years. They will continue producing fruit and flowers if you choose wisely and maintain them correctly.

How to design a small garden

If you have a courtyard garden, you can do a few design things to maximise your space and make the most of your yard. We discussed a few of these points above, but here are a few more tips to be mindful of when making a design plan.

1. Firstly, consider creating an overall structure for the garden, considering the different uses of space and designated areas. For example, you may want to commit to using your yard for one primary purpose and build around that. Having a clear vision will prevent you from unnecessarily adding clutter with garden elements you do not need. Furthermore, the 'zones' you create will make your space feel larger as you will feel like you have many outdoor rooms.

2. Secondly, make your garden boundaries work together to make the garden feel like a room. Even if you have a fence on one side and a natural boundary (such as a hedge or planting border) on the other, create some cohesiveness in your design so that they do not mismatch and overwhelm the

effect you are aiming for in your garden. Consider adding wall hangings to boundaries to tie them together.

3. Soften the edges of boundaries: Regarding boundaries, softening the edges of where walls meet floors will transform your small space into a welcoming garden. You can add plant containers on the edges of convergence points between the boundaries. Additionally, large containers can add structure and unity to your landscape. Boundaries can, unfortunately, make a small garden seem unhomely if not broken up visually; try using climbers and planting along the edges to eliminate the prison-like look.

4. Utilise the windowsill: As well as using containers to grow plants, why not use the kitchen windowsill? Window boxes are a clever way to increase planting in limited spaces and are perfect for growing herbs (especially if you use them in cooking).

5. Use screening sparingly: Remember that screening significantly reduces light if you want privacy in a small garden. Therefore, you should

only add it to your garden if blocking the view of nosy neighbours is a priority.

6. Consider your sun patterns: Speaking of shade, be careful where you place your hardscape; a tall structure may shade your house, which is incredibly unhelpful in less sunny months. You should also ensure you place seating areas in accordance with sun patterns. For example, if you live in a hot climate, you may want to be shaded to stay cool, whereas, in a cooler climate, you will want to be seated under the sun. (This is why site analysis is essential before you start designing).

7. Use small, medium, and large plants: For softscape, ensure you have a variety of sizes and forms - do not stick to small plants just because your garden is small, as this will highlight how small your space is. Using many sizes will add interest to your landscape. Additionally, layered planting works well in all gardens, so try to add levels to your planting to give your garden depth and the illusion of having more foliage.

8. Use neutral tones: Another design tip to make your garden feel bigger is to stick to neutral

colours rather than bold, bright ones. Dark colours may also make your garden seem darker than it is, so neutral tones are the way forward for garden basics. However, you can still add a pop of colour with more minor garden elements, like cushions for outdoor seating (and planting, of course). Also note that warmer colours make a space feel more intimate while cooler colours open up a space, adding depth.

9. Use reflections to your advantage: A ninth tip is to use garden mirrors. Like with interiors, you can use them to create an illusion of a bigger space. To blend it into the garden setting, layer a mirrored board with a trellis or use a garden gate mirror. Another advantage is enjoying a garden view from alternative areas utilising the reflection.

10. Use elevation: Tip number 10 is to use elevated furniture, such as a hanging chair. Elevated furniture will not break the line of sight since the floor is kept clear, making the space feel clearer. Hanging furniture also adds levels to your garden. Furthermore, creating levels in your garden through steps, ledges, or raised beds (to name a few examples) will open up the space and

add perspective.

11. Incorporate a fire pit: If you want to extend the enjoyment of your garden into the evenings, why not add a fire pit as a focal point? Fire pits work for any size garden and can add such cosiness to a more miniature garden.

12. Plant a multi-stemmed tree: Another idea for a focal point is to plant a multi-stemmed tree. A growing trend, these trees can create a statement in the garden and a simulated woodland environment.

Remember, having a small garden does not need to be restrictive. In fact, it forces you to be more creative, often resulting in many stylish and beautiful designs. Due to their size, they tend to be lower maintenance and more budget-friendly than bigger gardens.

General Design ideas

The following ideas will work well for any size garden, as it is design advice that will improve the look of your existing garden (or can be incorporated into your design plan to better it).

Let's start off with flooring. You should note that garden paving generally can dictate the layout and design of the whole garden. For example, to achieve a French country look, use grey or white stone in a random pattern, whereas laying out sandy-coloured stone in a mixed pattern emulates an English country feel. Therefore, ensure the way you lay your paving matches your overall design intent. You should also try to make your paving the same level as your indoor flooring for a seamless outdoor transition. The seamless flow also allows movement from your home to the garden.

The second idea is to make your lawn into a specific shape. Everything in your garden should be there because of your conscious choice. Therefore, if you have a lawn, consider shaping it into something that works with the rest of your garden. For example, a formal garden uses straight lines, so a rectangular or square lawn shape works best. But an informal garden may use more organic forms, inviting an oval or circular lawn shape. In any case, what matters is having a bold, clear choice. Shaping your lawn will show design intent and look more professional than leaving it to grow wild.

Thirdly, make everything work together by coordinating your colours, particularly your paving, with your plants. For example, purple and white flowers look stunning against grey or white stone; sunset tones of red, orange, and yellow look brilliant against strong black or silver paving; and pastel-toned flowers look lovely paired with golden pavers.

My next tip is for people with sloping gardens. If you want garden furniture, one effective way of levelling out your landscape is to apply decking to your garden. Decking will tolerate heavy footfall and will make a delightful dining area. Furthermore, decking can have split levels, adding visual interest to your garden.

Materiality is also crucial in tying your garden together. You can frame views, areas, or plants using certain elements found throughout the garden, such as timber posts. You may also have timber fences; this consistency in material choice will ensure a well-put-together look. For a touch of luxury, you could surround scented plants (such as lavenders and roses) with a flagstone terrace for a classic English garden style. Alternatively, combine the materials sandstone or limestone with minimalism and topiary.

When integrating a focal point, the best way to make it work for you is by nestling it with planting. For example, if you randomly place an ornament in the centre of your garden with no reason other than "it's in the middle", it will most likely look terrible; elements that are too small will get lost, and anything too large will overwhelm the garden.

So instead, frame your focal point into the surrounding landscape using your vegetation.

Incorporating a living wall is a superb idea for gardens of any size. It saves space, and vertical planting creates a dramatic yet eco-friendly addition to your garden that you can station anywhere. If installed against your home, it will regulate the temperature indoors, reducing energy costs. As an air purifier, a living wall is perfect for urban dwellers living near roadsides, simultaneously serving as a sound barrier.

The following design idea is brilliant for those of you who have children. No matter your garden size, you can incorporate a sense of play if you plan your design carefully. Think of it as a "hidden playground"; taking inspiration from Adolfo Harrison, you can integrate elements of play throughout your garden. For example, your stepping stones used for paving can double up as a playful element depending on how you lay them out; garden mirrors can add a sense of mystery and wonder; screening elements can aid in a game of hide and seek.

***

High-end garden ideas

We spoke so much about budget ideas and those that work for everyone. Now it's time to mention some luxury garden ideas for those with a bigger budget.

Suppose you want an area dedicated to well-being in your garden. Why not have a pool for exercise closely linked with a yoga and meditation area? This will provide beauty and functionality, as guests will love having a dip in the pool. Infinity-edge pools are particularly classy. The pool could be nearby an outdoor shower, and the yoga/meditation space can have seating for relaxation nearby. You could even add a sunken lounge area adjacent to the pool. To tie it all together, hint at small breakages in the space using planting and levels, such as decking.

A similar yet more budget-friendly way to add luxury to your garden is to include a water feature. As we now know, there are many types, but having marginal plants or clipped hedging on the edges of the water feature will create a beautiful reflection that takes your yard to a new level visually. The sound of flowing water provides your garden with a sense of calm, and depending on your water feature, it may also be used as a focal point. You will have a more dynamic yard by incorporating a water feature.

Garden art is a sure way to add luxury to your garden (and you do not necessarily need a large garden to make it work). When choosing a sculpture, ensure it is proportionate to the size of your yard; it will not overwhelm the rest of your garden elements or take up too much floor space. These are great when used as a focal point or at the end of a pathway. In a small garden, art will add focus (and make the yard seem bigger if placed at the end of a narrow edge). In a large garden, it will break up the space, possibly even acting as signposts. In terms of the best material to use, consider your regional climate when making a decision. Traditionally, natural and cast stones are used for sculptures as they age well, have incredible durability, and are frost-resistant. Of course, to keep the luxurious look, you should use planting as a backdrop to your garden art to help it stand out. Alternatively, choose planting that complements your yard art. Another way to accentuate your yard art is lighting; consider lighting for your sculptures to capture the eye at night and how the sun falls on them during the day. Lighting can heavily influence the mood of the space and the overall impact of your garden art and should not be forgotten. Visiting sculpture parks is an easy way to get inspiration for your garden's art.

The difference between having lights and not having them can take your yard from sub-par to luxury. Lighting is imperative to ensure you can enjoy your backyard at any time of the day, and it heavily affects the garden's ambience. Many lighting choices are available, including decorative options. Warm white light particularly has a welcoming luminosity.

Another way to add a touch of glamour to your yard is to choose lush, tropical plants; the typical large leaf span promotes a feeling of sanctuary in the garden. Tropical planting is especially fitting for those who live in hotter climates and can successfully grow architectural planting, like palm trees. Statement plants give the best visual effect in smaller gardens. As a standard landscape design principle, you should choose a mixture of plants for their form, size, texture, and structure. Having said all this, I firmly believe that choosing native planting will be best for you. You can find architectural and statement plants native to your region; it does not have to be tropical. You and your plants will be happier because natives require less maintenance, filling your garden with effortless vitality.

Suppose you have an existing patio (or plan to have one). In that case, the seating, lighting, and planting design are the key to making it luxurious. Pick sleek furniture that matches your overall colour scheme and materiality for seating. You can smartly frame seating using well-kept, elegant planting, and above all, well-lit (using lights strategically to give atmosphere to the seating area while accentuating any architectural plants).

If, after reading this section, you feel as though you cannot have luxury due to a small budget, think again. You can acquire many of these elements in your garden with a bit of creativity and smart swaps. For example, instead of massive, tropical planting, you may choose younger plants that are inexpensive to purchase yet grow rapidly to full size. Using the abovementioned techniques, you can also focus your energy, time, and money on creating one luxurious focal point, such as a seating area.

7
Conclusion

To conclude, there are nine principles of landscape design which are: proportion, unity, repetition, order, line, form, texture, colour, and visual weight. If followed correctly, these principles will undoubtedly produce a wonderfully designed garden. You now know what each of them means and how to implement them in your garden.

The garden can be broken down into two main components (hardscape and softscape), and you know that a well-balanced garden uses both elements. You also know that you can achieve different garden styles by making certain design choices; for instance, you can create a formal garden using straight lines and symmetry, and an informal garden using natural, curved lines.

In chapter two, we learned about the importance of setting a budget and making a colour scheme for your garden, as missing these steps can lead to a disastrous landscape design. We also learned about considering maintenance when choosing your garden elements and planting, and most importantly, meeting the needs of the users of your yard. Your irrigation plans are another crucial step in the design process that ensures you will never have to deal with a waterlogged garden again. The importance of garden lighting was highlighted in this chapter, not just for aesthetics but also for home security and safety. Not including a lighting plan in your design is a mistake you now know to avoid to create the best garden possible. Forgetting to consider your regional climate and local biodiversity is another mistake we know not to make, as well as not including home security and fire safety in your garden design. Designing in accordance with your climate is easier for maintenance in the long run, and will ensure that your plants live a healthier and happier life. You also learned how to properly analyse your yard for elements you can keep rather than starting afresh. This analysis saves time, money, and the environment because you use fewer resources and energy when you design sustainably. Of course, you could always hire a landscape professional to carry out specific tasks, especially if you are not well-equipped to do the whole garden yourself.

Speaking of site analysis, in chapter three, we covered the importance of getting to know your garden's current conditions before you start designing. Site analysis is the first and most crucial step in the design process; you will only create a successful garden if you complete this. We also learned the basic steps of getting started with your garden design once your analysis is done, including picking a garden theme, organising garden 'rooms' for different uses, and the relevance of home materiality in relation to your garden (you want to ensure that your garden matches with your existing material palette). In the design phase, there are also specific questions to ask yourself to know if your design plan will work with your yard. You should create a visual hierarchy in your garden using various landscape design principles such as focalisation and balance. Having a visual hierarchy is one characteristic of a successful landscape. So are connected spaces through visual elements, pathways, and materials.

In chapter four, we learned several ways to achieve a climate-conscious garden through careful design and planning. All it takes is making the correct choices, such as using native planting or xeriscaping if you live in an arid climate. We also covered landscaping for the opposite conditions (wet and shady climates), including a plant selection that thrives in both conditions. Designing with a climate-conscious mindset also means thinking laterally, expanding your options and considering what is best for your garden in your current climate. A great example we discussed was having alternatives to a grass lawn. Landscaping in this way will save you water and money while being environmentally friendly at the same time.

With global warming constantly threatening our livelihoods, you now know of a few planting options with a much slower burning rate should there be a wildfire where you live. Most of these are high-water content plants, such as succulents. Chapter four also covered many of your worst nightmares: poor drainage. You are now knowledgeable about how to prevent this from ever happening to you again using several techniques, including diverting runoff, encouraging infiltration, landscape grading, and building a dry well. Let's not forget the last takeaway from this chapter: weatherproofing your garden. Depending on where you live, you may experience quite severe wind, rain, sun, snow, or all of the above. Chapter four explains many ways to weatherproof your garden and protect your beautiful plants, regardless of the weather.

The next chapter covered an extremely relevant topic in today's climate: sustainable design. You should rethink your design plan if you are not designing your garden sustainably. Not only is designing this way better for the environment, but it is also easier and better for you overall. Sustainable design means using native plant selection; imitating nature; making provisions for wildlife; and conserving water. It also means creating your dream garden by reusing and upcycling home and garden elements that you already have. Additionally, being a sustainable designer means assessing your yard to see what you can keep rather than scrapping everything and starting afresh.

The last chapter hopes to inspire you with design ideas that suit your budget. You are now aware that you can transform your yard into something you have always dreamt of, no matter your yard size or budget. There are ideas that work for all gardens and budgets and ideas that you can adapt to work for your specific situation. We looked specifically at the different types of hardscape and softscape, explaining that some elements work better for bigger gardens while others will be valuable additions to smaller gardens. After reading chapter six, research which hardscape and softscape work best for you. There are varying prices on the market, and you may find the best deals by comparing retailers. You may even discover that your budget allows for certain elements you did not think you could afford. Chapter six also highlights garden ideas specifically for those of you on a tight budget; many of these ideas link to the concept of sustainable design.

Before finishing off, I want to reinforce the idea that you really can make your garden fantasy a reality with a well-thought-out design plan and thorough site analysis. Whether you have a courtyard garden or acres to play with, we both know your dream is achievable. Follow the steps in this book, make a plan you fall in love with, and you will be successful.

Lastly, please leave a review on Amazon if you benefitted from the knowledge in this book. Thank you.

Bibliography

1. Landscaping Network. (2022, January 26). *What is Landscaping?* https://www.landscapingnetwork.com/landscape-design/what-is.html

2. Hansen, G. (2010). Basic Principles of Landscape Design. In *IFAS* (No. CIR536). University of Florida. Retrieved February 14, 2023, from https://edis.ifas.ufl.edu/publication/MG086

3. Newman, A., & Obermiller, J. (2023). Understanding primary, secondary, and tertiary colors. *Adobe*. Retrieved February 17, 2023, from https://www.adobe.com/creativecloud/design/discover/secondary-colors.html

4. Schau, B. (2019, April 18). The Difference Between Hardscaping and Softscaping. *Landscape Solutions*. Retrieved February 18,

2023, from https://landscape-solutions.net/difference-between-hardscaping-and-softscaping/

5. Stoeckig Landscaping Group. (2020). 5 DIFFERENCES BETWEEN HARDSCAPE AND SOFTSCAPE. *Stoeckig Landscape Group*. Retrieved February 18, 2023, from https://stoeckiglandscapegroup.com/5-differences-between-hardscape-and-softscape/

6. Swift, J. & BBC Gardeners' World. (2021, July 27). *Three golden rules of garden design* [Video]. Gardeners' World. Retrieved February 18, 2023, from https://www.gardenersworld.com/how-to/grow-plants/nine-garden-design-tips/

7. Publishing, D. K., Griffiths, A., Keightley, M., Gatti, A., & Allaway, Z. (2020). *RHS Your Wellbeing Garden: How to Make Your Garden Good for You*. DK. https://books.google.co.uk/books?id=DzfSDwAAQBAJ&dq=how+to+design+your+garden&lr=&source=gbs_navlinks_s

8. Italy, C. (2022, October 9). Best Plants and Erosion Controls for Slopes and Hillsides. *Dengarden*. Retrieved February 20, 2023, from https://dengarden.com/landscaping/Good-Plants-and-Erosion-Controls-for-Slopes

9. Whittaker, L. (2019, April 12). *Home Security Landscaping Tips: Easy Ways to Make Your Home Safer | Install-It-Direct*. INSTALL-IT-DIRECT. https://www.installitdirect.com/learn/home-security-landscaping-tips-easy-ways-to-make-your-home-safer/

10. Whittaker, L. (2021, November 11). *25 Common Landscaping Mistakes and How to Avoid Them*. INSTALL-IT-DIRECT. https://www.installitdirect.com/learn/common-landscaping-mistakes-to-avoid/

11. Engels, J. (2022, March 18). *7 Reasons Why Reusing and Repurposing is Better than Recycling*. One Green Planet. https://www.onegreenplanet.org/lifestyle/why-reusing-and-repurposing-is-better-than-recycling/

12. Anderson, D. (2019, October 11). *Outdoor Landscape Lighting Tips & Ideas | Install-It-Direct*. INSTALL-IT-DIRECT. https://www.installitdirect.com/learn/outdoor-landscape-lighting-tips-ideas/

13. *ENH1112/EP375: Landscape Design: Ten Important Things to Consider*. (n.d.). https://edis.ifas.ufl.edu/publication/EP375

14. *ENH1165/EP426: Landscape Design: Analyzing Site Conditions*. (n.d.). https://edis.ifas.ufl.edu/publication/ep426

15. *CIR536/MG086: Basic Principles of Landscape Design*. (n.d.). https://edis.ifas.ufl.edu/publication/MG086

16. Kelly, T., & Fazzani, L. (2023, February 28). *55 low-cost ways to give your garden a new look without blowing the budget*. Ideal Home. https://www.idealhome.co.uk/garden/garden-ideas/budget-garden-ideas-197528

17. BBC Gardeners' World Magazine. (2022, October 22). *How to start a new garden*. https://www.gardenersworld.com/plants/how-t

o-start-a-new-garden/

18. *Create Privacy in Your Yard*. (2022, July 9). Better Homes & Gardens. https://www.bhg.com/gardening/design/styles/create-privacy-in-your-yard/

19. Titchmarsh, A. & Gardeners' World. (2019, July 20). *Watering plants effectively* [Video]. Gardeners'World.com. Retrieved March 1, 2023, from https://www.gardenersworld.com/how-to/maintain-the-garden/watering-plants-effectively/

20. BBC Gardeners' World Magazine. (2022a, September 8). *Dealing with drought in the garden*. https://www.gardenersworld.com/how-to/maintain-the-garden/dealing-with-drought-in-the-garden/

21. *How to Grow Thyme*. (2022, April 20). The Spruce. https://www.thespruce.com/how-to-grow-thyme-1402630

22. Mcintosh, J. (2022, July 13). *How to Grow and*

Care for Zoysia Grass. The Spruce. Retrieved March 1, 2023, from https://www.thespruce.com/zoysia-grass-plant-profile-4691117

23. Iannotti, M. (2022, July 30). *How to Grow Lavender: Planting and Care* (M. Leverette, Ed.). The Spruce. Retrieved March 1, 2023, from https://www.thespruce.com/growing-lavender-1402779

24. Puisis, E. (2021, July 13). *How to Grow and Care for Slipper Plants* (B. Gillette, Ed.). The Spruce. Retrieved March 1, 2023, from https://www.thespruce.com/slipper-plants-profile-5185750

25. Mcintosh, J. (2022a, May 3). *How to Grow and Care for Asters*. The Spruce. Retrieved March 2, 2023, from https://www.thespruce.com/perennial-aster-flower-plants-1316032

26. Iannotti, M. (2021, October 20). *How to Grow and Care for Coreopsis* (K. Miller, Ed.). The Spruce. Retrieved March 2, 2023, from

https://www.thespruce.com/growing-and-using-coreopsis-in-the-flower-garden-1402839

27. Beaulieu, D. (2021, November 3). *How to Grow and Care for Lamb's Ear* (M. Leverette, Ed.). The Spruce. Retrieved March 2, 2023, from https://www.thespruce.com/lambs-ears-uses-how-to-care-and-control-2132610

28. Iannotti, M. (2022a, June 2). *How to Grow and Care for Aloe Vera*. The Spruce. Retrieved March 2, 2023, from https://www.thespruce.com/grow-aloe-vera-1403153

29. Iannotti, M. (2022b, July 13). *How to Grow and Care for Artichokes* (D. Lagattuta, Ed.). The Spruce. Retrieved March 2, 2023, from https://www.thespruce.com/tips-for-growing-artichokes-1403455

30. Mcintosh, J. (2022a, April 30). *How to Grow and Care for Beardtongue (Penstemon)* (B. Gillette, Ed.). The Spruce. Retrieved March 3, 2023, from https://www.thespruce.com/penstemon-care-1316041

31. Taylor, L. (2022, November 28). *15 Best Plants for Drought-Tolerant Gardens* (S. Harris, Ed.). The Spruce. Retrieved March 3, 2023, from https://www.thespruce.com/water-wise-plants-drought-tolerant-gardens-2736715

32. Beaulieu, D. (2022, April 28). *How to Grow and Care for Purple Fountain Grass* (K. Miller, Ed.). The Spruce. Retrieved March 3, 2023, from https://www.thespruce.com/purple-fountain-grass-2132874

33. Michaels, K. (2022, February 24). *How to Grow and Care for Sweet Potato Vine* (J. Thompson-Adolf, Ed.). The Spruce. Retrieved March 3, 2023, from https://www.thespruce.com/sweet-potato-vines-4120149

34. Beaulieu, D. (2022, September 7). *How to Grow and Care for Trumpet Vine* (B. Gillette & E. Estep, Eds.). The Spruce. Retrieved March 4, 2023, from https://www.thespruce.com/stop-spreading-of-trumpet-vines-2132896

35. Myers, V. R. (2021, July 7). *How to Grow Blue Blossom Ceanothus*. The Spruce. Retrieved March 6, 2023, from https://www.thespruce.com/ceanothus-thyrsiflorus-growing-profile-3269246

36. Taylor, L. H. (2022, May 4). *The Best Drought Tolerant Lawn Alternatives*. The Spruce. Retrieved March 6, 2023, from https://www.thespruce.com/best-drought-tolerant-lawn-substitutes-2736710

37. Whittaker, L. (2019a, January 11). *Drought Resistant Landscaping*. INSTALL-IT-DIRECT. Retrieved March 6, 2023, from https://www.installitdirect.com/learn/drought-landscape-design/

38. Dillon, K. (2018, October 10). *10 Fire Safe Plants to Plant in the Garden | Install-It-Direct*. INSTALL-IT-DIRECT. https://www.installitdirect.com/learn/fire-safe-plants-to-consider-using-in-the-garden/

39. Burke, K. (2022, November 19). *Tips for Growing a Lawn in Dry Conditions*. The Spruce.

Retrieved March 8, 2023, from
https://www.thespruce.com/growing-lawn-in-dry-climate-2152856

40. Wallender, L. (2022, December 14). *12 DIY Yard Drainage Methods* (K. Bacon, Ed.). The Spruce. Retrieved March 8, 2023, from https://www.thespruce.com/diy-yard-drainage-methods-5080419

41. *Weather damage / RHS Gardening*. (n.d.). Royal Horticultural Society. Retrieved March 10, 2023, from https://www.rhs.org.uk/prevention-protection/weather-damage

42. BobVila.com. (2017, March 31). *10 Ways to Weather-Proof Your Garden*. Bob Vila. Retrieved March 10, 2023, from https://www.bobvila.com/slideshow/10-ways-to-weather-proof-your-garden-50980

43. Puisis, E. (2022, April 11). *How to Grow Blue Mistflowers* (D. Lagattuta & S. Scott, Eds.). The Spruce. Retrieved March 10, 2023, from https://www.thespruce.com/blue-mistflowers-g

uide-5188907

44. Puisis, E. (2022, March 23). *How to Grow and Care for Cardinal Flower* (J. Thompson-Adolf, Ed.). The Spruce. Retrieved March 10, 2023, from https://www.thespruce.com/growing-cardinal-flowers-5093922

45. Donnelly, C. (2022, May 30). *How to Grow and Care for New York Ironweed* (D. Lagattuta, Ed.). The Spruce. Retrieved March 10, 2023, from https://www.thespruce.com/new-york-ironweed-plant-profile-5069722#:~:text=New%20York%20ironweed%20(Vernonia%20noveborecensis,%2Dlying%20woods%2C%20and%20marshes.

46. *Osmunda regalis | royal fern Bogs/RHS Gardening*. (n.d.). Royal Horticultural Society. https://www.rhs.org.uk/plants/12001/osmunda-regalis/details

47. *Thelypteris palustris | ground fern Ferns/RHS Gardening*. (n.d.). Royal Horticultural Society. https://www.rhs.org.uk/plants/20658/i-thelypteris-palustris-i/details

48. Beaulieu, D. (2021, June 21). *Corkscrew Rush Plant Growing Profile*. The Spruce. Retrieved March 12, 2023, from https://www.thespruce.com/corkscrew-rush-plants-4125690#:~:text=Twisted%20or%20%22Corkscrew%22%20rush%20is,ability%20to%20spread%20via%20rhizomes.

49. Myers, V. R. (2021b, September 1). *Red Chokeberry Growing Tips*. The Spruce. Retrieved March 12, 2023, from https://www.thespruce.com/red-chokeberry-growing-tips-3269236

50. Sears, C. (2020, October 6). *How to Grow and Care for Black Huckleberries*. The Spruce. Retrieved March 12, 2023, from https://www.thespruce.com/how-to-grow-and-care-for-black-huckleberry-5076023#:~:text=Black%20huckleberries%20(Gaylussacia%20baccata)%20are,deep%20blue%2Dpurple%20edible%20berries.

51. Myers, V. R. (2022, June 15). *How to Grow and Care for Summersweet* (J. Thompson-Adolf, Ed.). The Spruce. Retrieved March 12, 2023,

from https://www.thespruce.com/how-to-grow-summersweet-3269223

52. Gardenia. (n.d.). *Rhododendron periclymenoides (Pinxterbloom Azalea)*. Gardenia Creating Gardens. Retrieved March 12, 2023, from https://www.gardenia.net/plant/rhododendron-periclymenoides

53. Beaulieu, D. (2022a, June 23). *How to Grow and Care for Mountain Laurel* (M. Leverette, Ed.). The Spruce. Retrieved March 12, 2023, from https://www.thespruce.com/mountain-laurel-plants-growing-tips-2131174

54. Iannotti, M. (2022, September 6). *How to Grow and Care for Black-Eyed Susan*. The Spruce. Retrieved March 13, 2023, from https://www.thespruce.com/choosing-and-growing-black-eyed-susan-1402860

55. Hicks-Hamblin, K. (2022, July 21). *15 of the Best Native Wildflowers for the US and Canada*. Gardener's Path. https://gardenerspath.com/plants/flowers/best-

native-wildflowers/

56. Price, M. (2022, July 7). *Plant Butterfly Weed for Pollinators*. Bay Weekly. Retrieved March 13, 2023, from https://bayweekly.com/plant-butterfly-weed-for-pollinators/

57. Christopher, T. (Ed.). (2011). *The New American Landscape*. Google Books. Retrieved March 13, 2023, from https://books.google.co.uk/books?hl=en&lr=&id=PpLOv5NLNCgC&oi=fnd&pg=PP2&dq=sustainable+garden+design&ots=K9FRDrlgI_&sig=1m0ZbP8Nu1Iwb7sTi3cG1FNsyWw&redir_esc=y#v=onepage&q=sustainable%20garden%20design&f=false

58. Vanderlinden, C. (2022, March 24). *How to Grow and Care for Butterfly Weed* (J. Thompson-Adolf & E. Step, Eds.). The Spruce. Retrieved March 13, 2023, from https://www.thespruce.com/growing-butterfly-weed-in-your-garden-2539531#:~:text=A%20type%20of%20milkweed%2C%20butterfly,late%20spring%20until%20late%20summer

59. Iannotti, M. (2022a, April 28). *How to Grow and Care for Common Yarrow* (J. Thompson-Adolf, Ed.). The Spruce. Retrieved March 13, 2023, from https://www.thespruce.com/achillea-growing-yarrow-in-the-perennial-garden-1402830

60. Gardeners' World. (n.d.). *Achillea millefolium*. BBC Gardeners World Magazine. Retrieved March 13, 2023, from https://www.gardenersworld.com/plants/achillea-millefolium/

61. McIntosh, J. (2022, September 23). *How to Grow and Care for Helenium (Sneezeweed)* (J. Thompson-Adolf, Ed.). The Spruce. Retrieved March 14, 2023, from https://www.thespruce.com/helenium-flowers-1316035

62. Georgia Native Plant Society. (2020, December 11). *Gray Goldenrod (Solidago nemoralis) - GNPS*. GNPS. https://gnps.org/plant/gray-goldenrod-solidago-nemoralis/#:~:text=Wildlife%3A,flies%2C%20beetles%2C%20and%20butterflies.

63. Beaulieu, D. (2022b, June 27). *How to Grow and Care for Goldenrod* (D. Lagattuta, Ed.). The Spruce. Retrieved March 14, 2023, from https://www.thespruce.com/goldenrod-wildflowers-2132951

64. *Jerusalem Artichoke (Helianthus tuberosus)*. (n.d.). Illinois Wildflowers. Retrieved March 14, 2023, from https://www.illinoiswildflowers.info/prairie/plantx/ja_sunflowerx.htm#:~:text=Jerusalem%20Artichoke%20is%20usually%20more,Halictid%20bees%2C%20and%20Andrenid%20bees.

65. Vanderlinden, C. (2022b, June 15). *How to Grow Jerusalem Artichokes* (J. Thompson-Adolf, Ed.). The Spruce. Retrieved March 14, 2023, from https://www.thespruce.com/how-to-grow-organic-jerusalem-artichokes-2539639#:~:text=Jerusalem%20artichokes%20(Helianthus%20tuberosus)%2C,of%20almost%20being%20considered%20invasive

66. *Allium cernuum | Sevenoaks Native Nursery*. (n.d.). Sevenoaks Native Nursery. Retrieved March 14, 2023, from

https://www.sevenoaksnativenursery.com/native-plants/perennials-and-bulbs/allium-cernuum/

67. Gardeners' World. (n.d.-b). *Allium cernuum*. BBC Gardeners World Magazine. Retrieved March 14, 2023, from https://www.gardenersworld.com/plants/allium-cernuum/

68. Iannotti, M. (2021, July 6). *How to Grow Purple Coneflower* (J. Thompson-Adolf, Ed.). The Spruce. Retrieved March 14, 2023, from https://www.thespruce.com/echinacea-purple-coneflowers-1402840#:~:text=Purple%20coneflower%2C%20or%20Echinacea%20purpurea,forgiving%20of%20dividing%20and%20transplanting

69. Backyard Ecology. (2019, June 11). *Purple coneflower (Echinacea purpurea)*. Retrieved March 14, 2023, from https://www.backyardecology.net/purple-coneflower/

70. Beaulieu, D. (2022c, September 6). *How to Grow and Care for Bee Balm* (J. Thompson-Adolf,

Ed.). The Spruce. Retrieved March 14, 2023, from https://www.thespruce.com/red-bee-balm-plants-2132327

71. Heath, O. (2018, December 3). *How to include wildlife in your garden design*. House Beautiful. Retrieved March 14, 2023, from https://www.housebeautiful.com/uk/garden/designs/a24852267/wildlife-garden-design/

72. Sweetser, R. (2021, December 21). *What Is Hugelkultur? Building the Ultimate Raised Bed*. Almanac.com. Retrieved March 15, 2023, from https://www.almanac.com/what-hugelkultur-ultimate-raised-bed

73. R. & Permaculture earth care, people care, future care. (2022, July 14). *The Many Benefits of Hugelkultur*. Permaculture. Retrieved March 15, 2023, from https://www.permaculture.co.uk/articles/the-many-benefits-of-hugelkultur/

74. Waddington, E. (2021, May 21). *How To Mimic Nature In Your Garden*. Polytunnel Gardening.

Retrieved March 15, 2023, from https://blog.firsttunnels.co.uk/how-to-mimic-nature-in-your-garden/

75. A. (2021, December 21). *Are Water Absorbing Crystals Good Plants? How To Use Them? | Your Indoor Herbs and Garden*. Your Indoor Herbs and Garden. Retrieved March 15, 2023, from https://www.yourindoorherbs.com/water-absorbing-crystal-for-indoor-herbs-do-you-need-them/

76. Littleton, S. (2018, July 20). *7 Smart Ways to Save Water in the Yard*. Bob Vila. Retrieved March 15, 2023, from https://www.bobvila.com/slideshow/7-smart-ways-to-save-water-in-the-yard-48742

77. Evans, S. (2022, November 8). An Introduction to Garden Ponds. Wharf Aquatics. Retrieved March 15, 2023, from https://wharfaquatics.co.uk/blogs/ponds/an-introduction-to-garden-ponds#:~:text=A%20garden%20pond%20or%20water,in%20almost%20any%20size%20garden.

78. *Create a log pile for wildlife | The RSPB*. (n.d.). The RSPB. Retrieved March 15, 2023, from https://www.rspb.org.uk/get-involved/activities/nature-on-your-doorstep/garden-activities/create-a-log-pile-for-wildlife/

79. Team, H. B. (2021, June 10). *16 garden design ideas to make the best of your outdoor space*. House Beautiful. Retrieved March 15, 2023, from https://www.housebeautiful.com/uk/garden/designs/a495/garden-design-ideas/

80. *"How to" Grow your Own with a VegTrug*. (2023, February 23). Perrywood. Retrieved March 17, 2023, from https://www.perrywood.co.uk/gardening-tips/grow-your-own/

81. Batty, D. (2022, October 27). *Bird and birdsong encounters improve mental health, study finds*. The Guardian. Retrieved March 17, 2023, from https://www.theguardian.com/environment/2022/oct/27/bird-birdsong-encounters-improve-mental-health-study

82. Kelly, T., & Fazzani, L. (2023, March 1). *55

low-cost ways to give your garden a new look without blowing the budget. Ideal Home. Retrieved March 17, 2023, from https://www.idealhome.co.uk/garden/garden-ideas/budget-garden-ideas-197528

83. Lush Garden Design. (2021, December 7). *Setting a budget for garden design | Lush Garden Design*. Retrieved March 17, 2023, from https://lushgardendesign.co.uk/design/setting-a-budget/

84. Doyon-Aitken, R., & Harley, C. (2020, March 5). *What's the Difference: Trellis, Arbor, and Pergola*. Fine Homebuilding. Retrieved March 18, 2023, from https://www.finehomebuilding.com/2009/05/01/whats-the-difference-between-a-trellis-an-arbor-and-a-pergola

85. Hansen, G. & IFAS University of Florida. (2019, September 26). *ENH1171/EP432: Arbor, Trellis, or Pergola—What's in Your Garden? A Mini-Dictionary of Garden Structures and Plant Forms*. UF IFAS Extension University of Florida. Retrieved March 19, 2023, from

https://edis.ifas.ufl.edu/publication/EP432

86. Team, H. B. (2019, January 12). *9 small garden design ideas on a budget*. House Beautiful. Retrieved March 21, 2023, from https://www.housebeautiful.com/uk/garden/designs/a1794/small-garden-ideas-budget/

87. Team, H. B. (2022, May 26). *22 cheap garden ideas for your outdoor space*. House Beautiful. Retrieved March 21, 2023, from https://www.housebeautiful.com/uk/garden/designs/g28/garden-ideas-on-a-budget/

88. Tilston, C. (2016, October 6). *Courtyard gardens: how to get the wow factor all year round*. House Beautiful. Retrieved March 22, 2023, from https://www.housebeautiful.com/uk/garden/designs/a873/courtyard-garden-maintenance/

89. Walsh, H., Parker, J., & Kelly, T. (2023, February 22). *38 Small garden ideas to maximise your outdoor space*. Ideal Home. Retrieved March 22, 2023, from https://www.idealhome.co.uk/garden/garden-id

eas/small-garden-ideas-2-174377

90. Tirelli, G. (2019, April 2). *Top 10 Benefits of Living Green Walls or Vertical Gardens*. Ecobnb. Retrieved March 24, 2023, from https://ecobnb.com/blog/2019/04/living-green-walls-benefits/

91. Team, H. B. (2021b, June 10). *16 garden design ideas to make the best of your outdoor space*. House Beautiful. Retrieved March 24, 2023, from https://www.housebeautiful.com/uk/garden/designs/a495/garden-design-ideas/

92. Crow, R. (2022, July 29). *Yard art ideas - 12 ways to enhance your space with sculpture or artwork*. homesandgardens.com. Retrieved March 26, 2023, from https://www.homesandgardens.com/gardens/yard-art-ideas

93. Crow, R. (2022a, July 29). *How do I add luxury to my backyard? 7 expert recommendations*. homesandgardens.com. Retrieved March 26, 2023, from https://www.homesandgardens.com/gardens/h

ow-do-i-add-luxury-to-my-backyard

94. Ebert, J., & Searle, L. (2022, August 29). *Backyard landscaping ideas – 25 elements your outdoor space needs*. homesandgardens.com. Retrieved March 27, 2023, from https://www.homesandgardens.com/ideas/backyard-landscaping-ideas

95. Van Leeuwen, H. (2016, May). *Top 6 Things to Consider for Your Garden | Van Leeuwen Green*. Van Leeuwen Green Plants Gardens Landscapes. Retrieved March 27, 2023, from https://www.vanleeuwengreen.com/blog/plant-selection-top-6-things-consider-garden

96. BBC Gardeners' World Magazine. (2021, July 27). Nine garden design tips. *GardenersWorld*. Retrieved February 18, 2023, from https://www.gardenersworld.com/how-to/grow-plants/nine-garden-design-tips/